LOUIS JORDAN

SON OF ARKANSAS, *Father of* R&B

STEPHEN KOCH

Charleston   London

THE
History
PRESS

Published by The History Press
Charleston, SC 29403
www.historypress.net

Front cover: Courtesy Library of Congress.
All photography courtesy Louise Terzia, from the author's collection, except as indicated.

First published 2014

Manufactured in the United States

ISBN 978.1.62619.435.9

Library of Congress CIP data applied for.

ABOUT THE AUTHOR

Arkansawyer Stephen Koch is a musician, playwright and award-winning reporter, editor and broadcast journalist. He's been studying the life and music of R&B pioneer Louis Jordan nearly since birth, getting hip to "Beans and Cornbread" bouncing on his dad's knee. He's spoken at and performed music in places ranging from the Rock and Roll Hall of Fame to festivals in the United Kingdom. Koch lives in Little Rock, where he is creator and host of *Arkansongs*, syndicated on National Public Radio affiliates.

Visit us at
www.historypress.net
....
This title is also available as an e-book

Louis Jordan has had a great and lasting influence upon my appreciation of music, and, perhaps, even my performance.
—RAY CHARLES

[Louis Jordan's] *impact in the '40s was comparable to that of the Beatles in the '60s.*
—LEONARD FEATHER

[Louis Jordan was] *a bridge between the blues and jazz.*
—SONNY ROLLINS

Louis Jordan's guitarist, Carl Hogan, was the inspiration for most of my solos.
—CHUCK BERRY

His talent was so awesome, I thought it had to be supernatural.
—JAMES BROWN

Here comes Louis Jordan, the new thing, and I jumped on the bandwagon. I got our group to sound like Louie and my work went up, just double, that quick.
—JACK MCVEA

CONTENTS

ACKNOWLEDGEMENTS

Pop, Mom, Mart, Louie, Martha, Drummer Tom, Berle, Cary DeVore, Peter Guralnick, Eugene Porter, Mara Leveritt, the Jacqueses, Tim Shaw, Bob Palmer, Bill Jones, Bill Sayger, Rick Dawson and all Zoltans, Vino's, KUAR, John Deering, Cliff F. Baker, Jana Frost, Bill G., Ian, Daniel and Jo Ellen of the Old State House Museum, Nancy Williams, El Buho, Zachariah, the Central Arkansas Library System, Levon Helm, Alvertis Isbell, Louise Terzia, Dee, Will, Lyn, Christen Thompson and Darcy Mahan of The History Press, Keith Merckx, Stephanie Smittle, free wi-fi and the Arkansas Department of Workforce Services Unemployment Services division.

AUTHOR'S NOTE

Louis Jordan and I go back as far as I can remember. But Louie has always been dead.

Though Louie himself and his time as a top entertainer were long gone, he was a star in my young mind. In the music-loving, disc jockey–helmed Arkansas Delta household in which I grew up, Jordan songs like "Rock Doc" and "Beans and Cornbread" were on my personal Hot 100. Driving through Brinkley, Arkansas, with the family as a child, I wondered where on earth the statue of the city's native son was located, especially since it wasn't in the most obvious place by my estimation: atop a pedestal in a roundabout on the main drag. Imagine my youthful horror to learn that such a statue did not exist, and that most people, even in Brinkley, had never heard of Louis Jordan.

I am conversely proud and humbled that through some of my own efforts and the efforts of many others, there actually is a bust of Louie now in his hometown, and many more people in Arkansas and beyond now know him. I've written numerous newspaper and magazine articles on Louie, some of which can be found in different forms within this book, and wrote Louie's biographical entry for the University of Arkansas Press's *Arkansas Biography*. I subsequently expanded that bio for the Arkansas Studies Institute's *Encyclopedia of Arkansas History and Culture*. On my syndicated radio show, *Arkansongs*, I've written several programs exploring his songs and staged Jordan tribute concerts in Little Rock for more than a decade. Somehow, I wrote and appeared in a Jordan stage musical based on Louie called *Jump!*, as well as a documentary film, *Is You Is: A Louis Jordan Story*. In the strangest of places, I've performed Louie's songs and preached the gospel of Jordan. Around the world, I'm reminded of the greatness of his music. Louie has taken me to a lot of places over the years, helped introduce me to some wonderful people—including his widow, Martha—and given me music and memories of my own.

As with the brash youthful vision that couldn't understand the lack of a Louie-as-Lenin edifice in Brinkley, it is with a similar naïveté that I hope this book will serve as some belated thankfulness to the man, his music, his musicianship and his influence. The Maestro with a Beat, the King of the Jukeboxes, the Godfather of R&B and the Original Rock 'n' Roller—here comes Mr. Jordan! Mop! Mop!

—S.K., Little Rock, Arkansas, U.S.A.

Note: Louis Jordan pronounced his first name "LEW-ee," not "LEW-is," and, early in his career, was even billed as "Louie Jordan." In that spirit, this book refers to Mr. Jordan as "Louie" throughout.

PROLOGUE

February 4, 1975
Los Angeles, California

L ouis Jordan, father of R&B, thought he'd take a nap.
   He was tired. There'd been some heart trouble recently but also invitations to work. He knew the doctor said he couldn't play saxophone, but he could still sing. Singing was good enough for festival bookers, but would people accept *the* Louis Jordan with only his golden voice—and not his silver saxophone? Would the house bands be able to hit the notes?

For so many years, he had rigidly controlled his own notes and the notes played by his musicians. It had worked even better for him than it had for his father. Louie had conquered the world in many ways, he sometimes thought, even in his own humbleness. Fifty top ten hits. Concert attendance records. TV and film appearances. International tours. From the moment he'd started playing music as a young boy, his musician dad had been tough on him and shown him that entertaining people was a business—a science— to be respected. He had learned the lessons so well that some musicians later couldn't get behind his zeal for perfection. He had dealt with that accordingly and figured those slackers deserved their own musical fates.

But things hadn't been great lately. Beyond the health problems, he hadn't been able to make a hit in a long while. The slump had turned into a trend, and by the 1960s and 1970s, he couldn't blame it on the novelty of rock 'n' roll anymore. He wasn't happy that Martha had to work, but she was the best money manager of all the wives he'd had. He didn't party his money away and liked that Martha didn't either. Sixty-six years old. It had all happened so fast. The days back home in Arkansas with his dad and aunt and uncle. Fishing. Baseball. Being a musician, of course. The hit parade. Movies. Then, just as fast, it seemed like it was all gone.

Except for Martha. Earlier that day, he'd told her he loved her today, as he did every day, and that he felt better today than he'd felt in a long time.

Louie rolled off the bed and hit the floor. Dimly, he could hear Martha going into hysterics on the phone. Then, dimmer still, her screaming out in the street while waiting for the paramedics. Finally, they came. But it was too late.

And after that, Martha almost went crazy.

Chapter 1

"I WAS DOING PRETTY GOOD THEN"

Louis Thomas Jordan was born on July 8, 1908, in Brinkley, Monroe County, Arkansas, United States of America.

Things were changing in the first years of the new century. Norway split with Sweden; Australia was formed. Albert Einstein's theory of relativity was published. In America, the Model T Ford was introduced, air travel was finally being worked out and the first radio broadcast took place.

Things weren't changing quite as fast where Louis Jordan came into being, but it was still buzzing. Monroe County is in the southeast part of Arkansas, in the state's Mississippi River Delta region, with plenty of wetlands, woods and incredibly flat land. Brinkley sits in the north part of Monroe County. With a population of around five thousand in 1908, it was one of the hub towns. Farming was the main industry when businesses, churches and hotels lined the dirt streets, as it remains today. People come from all around on Saturdays to shop, be seen and just get off the farm for a while. The nearby White and Cache Rivers still transport goods and people, as did the many trains going through the town proper. The cultivated delta land outside town is rich and dark, with its table-like horizon showcasing sunrises and sunsets much like the ocean.

The east Arkansas summers can be brutally humid, the winters freezing and wet. In between is tornado season. Louie wasn't yet one year old when a strong tornado hit Brinkley in March 1909 and ripped apart the town. Only a handful of buildings were left standing. The city was rebuilding as Louie grew into a boy.

He had already faced the death of his mother, Adell, when he was an infant. His grandmother Maggie Jordan took him in. She tolerated his honking beginnings on clarinet better than she did the trombone, which she made him play outside.

"I had a funny grandmother," Louie told radio station KFI in 1971. "She didn't like that blaring sound, so I had to drop it. She made me rehearse in the backyard. My father was on the road with a show so when he came back into town he brought a thirteen-key Albert-system clarinet. She let me practice that in the house providing I didn't play it in the high register—so that's the beginning of me playing the reeds. After I practiced clarinet for about six months, I got so I could play up high, then she wouldn't bother. I was doing pretty good then."

"My grandmother taught me that unless someone hit you, words cannot hurt you," Louie reflected in 1973. "I've been called anything you can think of, but it never offended me, and maybe that's one of the reasons why I got along so well in the South with the conditions like that."

When his grandmother died, Louie moved in with his aunt Lizzie and uncle Mack Reid on North Main Street in Brinkley. His father, Jim, stayed near the modest wood home when not on the road as a musician. James Jordan was born on June 16, 1876, in Dardanelle, Yell County, Arkansas, a port town along the Arkansas River. It's about 150 miles west of Brinkley, with Little Rock lying southerly between, and with the area's rolling hills, it is vastly different from Brinkley's flat delta.

Music was everything to James Jordan. He'd studied under W.C. Handy and toured with minstrel shows since young adulthood. Jim briefly abandoned touring for domesticity after Louie was born but soon rejoined F.G. Huntington's Mighty Minstrel Show, based out of Belzoni, Mississippi. The multi-instrumentalist spent much of the year on the road but kept Brinkley as his base. Music would soon have the same hold on his only son, Louie.

In an interview less than two years before his death, Louie told of his musical origins in a story that is cinematic if not apocryphal: "It was a saxophone in a store window. I could see myself in the polished brass—that started me off. I ran errands all over Brinkley until my feet were sore, and I saved until I could make a down payment on that shiny instrument. My father taught me music."

The Brinkley Brass Band formed in town when Louie was seven, and Jim became the band's founding teacher. At home, there was more music. Aunt Lizzie played piano for Brinkley's Mount Olive Baptist Church and gave lessons. Later, his father recruited his promising clarinetist son and other youngsters to join the Brinkley Brass Band due to vacancies caused by World War I. Under the shadow of his father's ever-raised eyebrow, Louie learned the worth of rehearsal—which later shaped bandleader Louie's strict musical values.

Louie also claimed to be the champion Charleston dancer in town. When his dancing wasn't allowed at a church program, he sang "I'm My Mamma's Little Boy" instead, proving he had a voice nearly as strong as his hoofing and reed playing. Despite his musical and performing acumen, it was plain he wasn't excelling in more academic pursuits. He'd already left the more rigorous Consolidated White River Academy for the Marion Anderson School.

Meanwhile, the uniformed Brinkley Brass Band toured by train all over the state and to nearby Tennessee and Missouri playing picnics, weddings, funerals, churches, Masonic lodges and more, usually just for expenses and the spreads of food that were put out for the musicians. Louie was featured on clarinet and, later, saxophone. It was something Louie would get used to—playing a wide variety of music for a wide variety of audiences.

Chapter 2

"GENERAL UTILITY ENTERTAINER"

With all this instruction and playing, teenaged Louie was becoming adept at reed instruments and reading music. So much so that when Jim, touring with the Rabbit Foot Minstrels, learned of a vacancy in the troupe, he thought his son could make the cut. The job—for clarinetist and "general utility entertainer"—sure sounded like Louie. He got the gig. It paid seventeen dollars a week.

Even among the traveling troupes, the Rabbit Foot show was well regarded and boasted names that would become legendary in popular music: Ma Rainey, Bessie Smith, Ida Cox, Rufus Thomas and, of course, Louis Jordan.

"The minstrels put up a tent, like a circus, and did the show from a platform," Louie recalled a half century later. "We had our own car in the train to carry the tent, and we had people put it up. After they got the tent up, we'd make a parade through the town. That night, we'd put on the show and pack up the tent and get out to the next town. We traveled sometimes two or three hundred miles. All over the south, and as far up as St. Louis and as far down as Florida. I got my food and a berth in the car, the seventeen dollars was clear. And at night the show was over about 11 o'clock, so we played dances in the town with eight or nine pieces from the 23-piece show band. We'd split $150 a week from the dances."

Like his dad, Louie, too, was now splitting his time between Brinkley and touring. Never a great student at anything except music, he began concentrating more on his craft. Music rarely left his mind. He also played in nearby Helena with the Dixie Melody Syncopators, which performed for customers at Helena's Dixie Drugstore. He worked for a grocer near his Main Street home, for a druggist and carrying travelers' bags from the train station to the nearby hotel. When he wasn't working or rehearsing, Louie liked baseball, fishing and clowning. But it was known he had his quiet, introspective moments.

"I tell you, playing the blues was my basic idea of music," he would say late in life. "Pick out some of my tunes that made it for millions—all of them based on the 12-bar blues."

In 1925, Louie toured with the Silas Green from New Orleans show. Also new was the C-melody saxophone Louie had gotten himself. He'd be playing sax as well as clarinet on this show, and he liked the new instrument.

Another Rabbit Foot tour followed. However, when 1927's Rabbit Foot tour ended, Louie decided not to return to his hometown but to hit the big city—Little Rock. He enrolled, but rarely attended, Arkansas Baptist College on High Street. He got part-time work playing with James "Brady" Bryant's Salt and Pepper Shakers. He'd intended to study music at the college but instead learned by experience. He began playing with bands along Little Rock's Ninth Street and elsewhere in the area and taking most of his solos with his new alto saxophone. The alto had replaced the C-melody as his preferred instrument. Ninth Street, known as "the Line," and environs were the city's black entertainment and business districts. In addition to grand ballrooms and small pool halls, there were beauty parlors, law offices, movie theaters, restaurants and more to attract patrons from well beyond city limits.

But things were booming in the south Arkansas oil towns of Smackover and nearby El Dorado, several miles north of the Louisiana state line. It was said they were paying musicians twice the Little Rock rate—although it may have been twice as tough as playing Little Rock. With teeming thousands in the area looking to make it rich, ramshackle, volatile entertainment districts of saloons, dance halls and houses of ill repute were quickly erected amidst the oil boom chaos. The clapboard sidewalks were just as crowded with humanity of every stripe as the muddy roads were with people, mules, wagons and carts. Alcohol, blood and other bodily fluids flowed through the dirt streets.

Louie had a job within hours.

The musical selections weren't always great, but the tips usually were. Besides, Louie was in his element and, as always, eager to learn from other musicians. He'd long since learned to make audiences happy, but with these rough-and-tumble crowds, such a mindset was especially important, and vital to one's health. He played with Jimmy Pryor's Imperial Serenaders, and when that band imploded, he and some bandmates formed another group, Bob Alexander's Harmony Kings.

Louie felt doubly obligated to work, as he'd gotten married. Her name was Julia, but she went by Julie and was from Arkadelphia, in Clark County in southwest Arkansas. She was pregnant and gave birth to a daughter, Patty. Louie later found out Patty wasn't his, though he apparently later helped support her to a degree.

Louie came a bit late to the oil party as well. As the south Arkansas oil flow reduced to a trickle, so did the money.

Chapter 3

"TELL-'EM-'BOUT-ME"

The band took a months-long residency at a club in Hot Springs, Arkansas. The steaming natural hot springs in the southwest part of the state had drawn people from all over since well before statehood. Just like Native American tribes were said to have done in the area centuries before, rival gangland Prohibition-era factions set down their weapons in this neutral ground to frolic and relax.

At the turn of the twentieth century, Hot Springs was being billed as the "Carlsbad of America" for its bathhouses, resorts and scenery. By the 1930s, the tourist town was just as known for its gambling, prostitution, liquor and drugs as its water, although its official slogan was "We Bathe the World." There was also an ostrich farm, an alligator farm, an amusement park and burro rides to the observation tower at the top of the mountain nearby to enjoy—and of course, the city's thriving music and nightclub scene. Hot Springs offered near-equal excitement without the anarchy of the oil towns down south—while Brinkley offered less of all the above. Authors, boxers, baseballers, horse jockeys, statesmen, outlaws, entertainers and invalids alike visited Hot Springs to partake of its healing waters and amenities. The city's international visitors and cosmopolitan flavor meant American Jim Crow laws weren't always enforced to the strictest measure. Still, when the residency at Lucious Wilson's Tell-'Em-'Bout-Me Café ended, the band members went their separate ways.

Louie stayed in Hot Springs. He sent for Julie and Patty and rented a room at Pleasant and Garden Streets. It was a nice neighborhood where many of the black service workers of the city's nightclub, gambling and bathhouse trades lived. Just a couple of blocks away were the opulent bathhouses of the main thoroughfare, Central Avenue, called Bath House Row. Louie still visited home in Brinkley and was initiated into Brinkley's black Providence Masonic Lodge #36 at his father's urging. Back in Hot Springs, Louie played at Wilson's Tell-'Em-'Bout-Me Café, the Eastman Hotel and the Woodman of the Union Hall. But at some point, Julie, with her hometown nearby, left Hot Springs—as well as Louie.

Louie scored a good gig when he joined the wife and husband–led band of pianist Ruby "Junie Bug" Williams and drummer Selmer "Tuna Boy" Williams at the Green Gables club. The band then established an even better residency at the plush Club Belvedere, a structure maintaining a functional elegance as part of a country club golf course nearly a century later. Louie continued impressing bandmates and listeners alike with his musical prowess and showmanship. Even after gigs, Louie kept studying—obsessively listening to the radio and other bands. It paid off on the bandstand.

Among those who noticed Louie's talent was a vacationing performer from yet another traveling show, Dr. Sells's Traveling Medicine Show. Texas-born singer-dancer Ida Fields and Louie met at a promotional cakewalk parade put on by Lucious Wilson of Tell-'Em-'Bout-Me fame, where Louie was freelancing after season's end at the Belvedere. Dr. Sells himself and his wife, also relaxing in Hot Springs from their show, were persuaded to hear this dynamic and versatile singer and reed player. Sure enough, Louie was invited to join the troupe and traveled to the next Dr. Sells show in Pennsylvania. They stopped by Brinkley on the way north so Louie could gather some things and say goodbye.

Louie later explained it this way: "At that time, it was a big thing for the ballplayers to come down to Hot Springs. A lot of people come down to see them work and get in shape and they heard me play. A couple of guys said, 'Man, we ought to take this cat out East.'"

Louie didn't work out with the medicine show, but things seem to have gone better with Fields—the two became a couple. She was born in Texas, was six years older than Louie and had been a member of a traveling dancing troupe called the Florida Orange Blossoms. To Louie, she was worldly and knowledgeable about show business. Louie and Fields married in 1932 and got an apartment at 705 South Fifteenth Street, although he was still apparently married to Julie.

"He never said nothing about no wife," Fields later said.

From there, they went to Philadelphia, Pennsylvania, where Louie joined the Charlie Gaines band, one of the city's top bands. He also joined the musicians' union, Local 274 of the American Federation of Musicians. Soon after, the Gaines band got the opportunity to briefly tour with Louis Armstrong and record with him in Camden, New Jersey. The recording session was a medley of Armstrong's previous hits, ably backed but unremarkable. More notable was that this was the first pairing of Louis Armstrong and Louie Jordan. In a decade, they would return to the studio to duet together as equals. But at this point, Louie was happy to have a job, and the Armstrong session was a plum.

Still flush with touring and recording with a known name like Louis Armstrong, Louie got to record his own first solo vocal. "I Can't Dance, I Got Ants in My Pants" was a Charlie Gaines song that bandleader and publisher Clarence Williams asked to record with Gaines and Jordan. They did, in nearby New York City, in 1934. Jordan's vocal sounds as lively and assured as it would on future Chick Webb releases.

Louie's long rehearsals, plainly evident talent, charisma and persistence were paying off. He was also meeting and impressing the right people. Ralph Cooper with Harlem's Apollo Theatre—who would end up doing Amateur Night at the Apollo for a half century—saw Louie playing in Philadelphia. Cooper liked his ballad singing, sax playing and stage presence and told Louie that he should relocate to New York City, where more things were happening—specifically, a job in the Apollo house band. Louie didn't need much convincing; neither did Ida.

Louie spent most of 1935 going back and forth between the two cities, establishing himself and getting his New York union membership in Local 802. (Turns out, he couldn't work a steady job like the Apollo band without a six-month cooling-off period and subsequent transfer of his membership in Philadelphia's Local 274.)

He remained close with Gaines and worked with drummer/bandleader Joe "Kaiser" Marshall as well as bandleader LeRoy Smith, both of whom toured and featured Louie in their shows. In March 1936, the Smith band headlined the Apollo. "That was a big band that played strictly Paul Whiteman's style," Louie would say about LeRoy Smith's band. "Real high class music. In fact, I was the only one allowed to play some jazz once in a while and do a little singing."

But none of this could compare to the boost that being in the Chick Webb band could bring.

William Henry "Chick" Webb discovered Louie from hearing "I Can't Dance, I Got Ants in My Pants," which Webb's band had covered. Webb, a drummer and bandleader, had also heard Louie when he filled in for a sick member of the famed Apollo house band in Harlem and had then sent someone to see Louie when he was in Philadelphia. The Chick Webb Orchestra was one of the most prominent bands of the 1930s, and to be considered to join Webb's group illustrated how good a musician and showman Louie had become.

Webb's birthdate is in dispute, but he was close in age to Louie—Webb's tombstone lists 1909 as the birth year. Fellow jazz drummer Buddy Rich later called Webb the "daddy of them all," while Gene Krupa credited Webb with bringing drummers to the fore in jazz bands. Duke Ellington helped Webb get his first gig in the mid-1920s—and later appropriated Webb's sidemen Johnny Hodges and Charles "Cootie" Williams. Webb was known for his humor, temper and ability to tell tall tales.

Webb's drumming skills were all the more notable due to his being hunchbacked and rarely in good health. The Chick Webb Orchestra was doing great, but Webb himself was not a well man. Deformed with spinal tuberculosis, Webb had had this and other related health problems since he was a child and often played in pain. By the late 1930s when Louie joined, Webb had begun taking health breaks from leading his namesake band.

· · · · · · · · · · · · · · · · · · · ·

"I started playing gigs with Kaiser Marshall," Louie later recalled, "and we'd play over in Jersey and upstate in Connecticut and Massachusetts. And we kept on playing around until my six months was up and I could get in the union, so I could play a steady job. And that's when I met Chick Webb. At that time, Ella [Fitzgerald] wasn't with Chick. She won the contest on the amateur hour at the Apollo and then Chick picked her up. And then, two months after he picked her up, he come and got me."

Ella Fitzgerald was still a teenager when she joined the Webb band. Webb didn't dispel the untrue notion that he and his wife had adopted Fitzgerald; he thought it was good publicity. Her first recording with the Webb band—or with anyone—was the summer of 1935's "Love and Kisses."

Fitzgerald's role in the band soon became more prominent. In fact, her popularity helped change the entire band dynamic of the era, giving the lead vocalist more prominence when he or she had previously been relegated to a few feature songs scattered throughout the show.

Louie, too, was impressed with Fitzgerald, and the first recordings Louie did as a Webb sideman featured her. In January 1937, he and Fitzgerald formed part of a vocal trio on "There's Frost on the Moon," while Louie

Chick Webb and His Orchestra's "Clap Hands! Here Comes Charlie" from 1937 features Louis Jordan on saxophone and ranks among Jordan's earliest recordings.

recorded a solo vocal on "Gee, But You're Swell." In March, Louie was featured vocalist on "It's Swell of You" and "Rusty Hinge" while again being part of a vocal trio with Fitzgerald on "Wake Up and Live" and was featured sax soloist on "That Naughty Waltz" and "Clap Hands! Here Comes Charlie."

"Rusty Hinge" in particular offers an early glimpse at what would become the hallmarks of a classic Jordan side: Louie portraying a swinging, boozy "good for nothing" hepcat "on a binge." In reality, Louie was a reserved, solitary and near-teetotaling Baptist, the polar opposite of the jiving boozehound letting the good times roll on records that would, for better or worse, make his musical reputation.

In addition to touring and its Decca Records recordings, Webb's orchestra could be heard on radio broadcasts around the United States and as far away as Europe via short wave. Fitzgerald, who had also gotten her own deal with Decca, continued to delight crowds with her angelic warbling. Her "A-Tisket, A-Tasket" had become a big hit for the group.

Meanwhile, *Down Beat* magazine critic John Hammond, in a November 1937 article, criticized Webb's "elaborate, badly written 'white' arrangements" and a perceived low standard of musicianship for the band. He took a moment to dismiss particularly the efforts of the band's "'comedian' saxophonist." Hammond didn't even deign to mention Louie's name in the story; it wouldn't be the last time Louie would be so characterized.

Louie continued to be intrigued by Fitzgerald professionally and personally, even as she cut into his own stage time. The single Fitzgerald and the doubly married Louie romanced through the summer until Louie left the band. Fitzgerald was Webb's star attraction but not yet in possession of much stage presence, so Louie played an important part of the show by interacting with the audience, along with band emcee Bardu Ali. Ali "conducted" the band between doing tumbling stunts—John Hammond had dismissed him as "an athletic director who mimes around and contributes not a whit to the proceedings." Despite the detractors, with Fitzgerald leading the way, Webb's band was more popular than ever. Webb was taking frequent breaks as his health deteriorated. Louie, "comedian saxophonist," and trumpeter Taft Jordan, no relation, shared fronting the band in Webb's absences, with Ali emceeing.

But Louie had designs to create his own band and put out the idea to bandmates Fitzgerald, Taft Jordan and bassist Beverly Peer. The three were understandably reluctant to leave the successful Webb orchestra to join a quantity even less known than themselves. Webb was not amused—he fired Louie, though the exact cause has been cited as both Louie's would-be theft of band members as well as what's been called his "upstaging" of Fitzgerald. Webb apparently had been aware of their affair, but Louie attempting to start a band with Fitzgerald was another matter entirely.

Little more than a year later, on June 16, 1939, Webb was dead. It was said he died in his mother's arms and, if his Baltimore tombstone is to be believed, at age thirty. The band was touring in Alabama with a substitute drummer at the time. Though the audience was said to have heard the news of Webb's death at the time of the show, the band hadn't been informed—and the band didn't understand the subdued audience reaction as the show progressed until later.

In a matter of weeks, the Webb band was Fitzgerald's. Over the years, Louie never admitted to interviewers that he was fired from the band,

While Dizzy Gillespie (left) looks dreamy in this 1947 Ella Fitzgerald photograph, Tympany Five bassist Milt Jackson (at right) is all business. Louis Jordan and Fitzgerald had a romantic as well as a professional relationship and recorded several duets following their time together with Chick Webb. *Courtesy William P. Gottlieb/Ira and Leonore S. Gershwin Fund Collection, Music Division, Library of Congress.*

maintaining that he was in the orchestra up until Webb's death and glossing over the "lost year." In fact, Louie claimed in the 1970s that he asked Webb to get him a solo recording date, "and he said he would and I kept on asking him, so he just said, 'Well, I believe I will get him one, just to stop him from asking me.' So he asked Decca to record me, and that's how I got started."

But the truth was, Louie now had little to lose in starting his own band. Still, leading a band of his own wasn't a lark.

"Before I got a band, I knew what I wanted to do with it," he recalled in the early 1970s.

"I wanted to give my whole life to making people enjoy my music. Make them laugh and smile. So I didn't stick to what you'd call jazz. I have always stuck to entertainment."

Beyond scheming to take some Webb band members, he'd already alerted a drummer, Walter Martin—taking lessons on the tympani drums from Saul Goodman of the New York Philharmonic Orchestra—to get ready. Louie had heard a band using tympani drums live and decided they were a good stage gimmick. Ida began making payments on a set of the drums, which can change pitch with a foot pedal. While they rehearsed their debut, Louie took a gig playing with Edgar Hayes's band around New York City. Trumpeter Chester Boone and pianist Clarence Johnson rounded out the band, which started its first residency at the Elks Rendez-Vous in Harlem, New York, getting the gig following a tip from Ralph Cooper.

"Nine pieces," Louie asserted in July 1973, "and we had a regular gig at the Elks Rendez-Vous. 464 Lenox Avenue was the address. Also played club dates and 'off nights.' Those were nights when a band was off. I played up and down Swing Street, Fifty-Second Street. After a while, I cut the nine pieces down to six. Later I added guitar and made it seven. Once I got known as Louis Jordan and His Tympany Five, I kept the name. But [inflating his band numbers] I always had seven or eight men."

The purposeful misspelling of "tympani" would be used throughout Louie's career, as would the name the Tympany Five—no matter how many musicians were in the band. The actual tympani drums would later be dropped from the act. The band's first gig was August 4, 1938. Louie had just turned thirty.

Just as quickly, the band got the chance to record, backing Rodney Sturgis, a favorite vocalist at the Elks Rendez-Vous. Louie started adding more rehearsals to the band's schedule, though money was already tight. Trumpeter Boone balked and quit—the first in a long line of Tympany Five members who would tire of the long rehearsals and leave or get fired. Courtney Williams, fresh off the road with Fats Waller's big band, replaced him. Jordan added bassist Charlie Drayton into the mix, making the Tympany Five actually number five men for the first time.

"After that Fifty-Second Street bit," Louie recalled in the same 1973 interview, "I started playing proms, like at Yale and Amherst. That's when friends began saying, 'Why don't you get out of New York, Louis? It's taking too long for you to get started.' So they came and asked me if I would play with the Mills Brothers in Chicago. The Capitol Lounge was for white folks. It was across the alley from the Chicago Theater. Not many Negroes came to play because they felt they weren't welcome. They wanted me to play intermission for the Mills Brothers. I started not to go—that was a big mistake. At first I was doing ten minutes, then they raised me to fifteen, then I got to half an hour…After that booking, I was gone!"

Things were coalescing for the nascent bandleader and his dream of a crack outfit that played sharp and looked sharp—a small band that could sound as big as a big band.

The group's initial recordings were billed as by Rodney Sturgis with Louis Jordan's Elks Rendez-Vous Band and, on the numbers recorded without Sturgis during the session, as by Louis Jordan's Elks Rendez-Vous Band. One of the two, "Honey in the Bee Ball," was written by Louie and had become the band's theme. "Barnacle Bill the Sailor," with its humorous tale of an amorous sailor and the boys responding to lyrics in girly high-pitched voices, was a harbinger of many a Tympany Five novelty number to come.

Things went so well with the recordings that Jordan and the band were contracted to do more for Decca. That March—finally billed as Louis Jordan and his Tympany Five—the band cut six sides. There were two tympani-featuring instrumentals, "Flat Face" and "Swingin' in the Cocoanut Tree," the tympani-accented "Sam Jones Done Snagged His Britches," "Keep A-Knockin,'" "At the Swing Cat's Ball" and Louie's own "Doug the Jitterbug."

With its tale of a numbers-playing "viper" (a marijuana smoker in hepcat parlance) in "Sam Jones Done Snagged His Britches," of a swinging party in "At the Swing Cat's Ball" and of a dancing fool in "Doug the Jitterbug," some of the material sounded straight out of the Cab Calloway songbook. Beyond the incredible apprenticeship he'd had growing up, as Louie's musical circumstances improved, he continued to study the showmanship nuances of the likes of Calloway, Fats Waller and Louis Armstrong offstage.

Briefly billing himself as the "modern Bert Williams," Louie obviously self-identified with the song and stage man, who was popular when Louie was younger. Tellingly, Williams had a gift with humorous songs and bits of stagecraft and won wide fortune and acclaim through his ability to appeal to white audiences in the segregated United States. Louie was still refining his sound, but these were among the elements he would alchemize to make his own.

"Doug the Jitterbug" and "Keep A-Knockin'"—later covered memorably by Little Richard—were also released in Britain, Louie's first exposure overseas. The Europeans would soon be as crazy for Louie as the Americans. Other lands would follow.

In his autobiography, Mezz Mezzrow quotes the original, bawdy "Keep A-Knockin'" lyrics, as sung from the point of view of a prostitute too busy working to answer the door: "That number is a wonderful example of what happened to the blues when they moved out of the gallion, the work-gang and the levee and rode the rods into big towns…The Negroes who hit these cities found themselves on the bottom of the pile, on an even level with practically nobody but whores and sporting people…It often happened that a man who migrated into town couldn't eat unless his woman made money off other men…Many a guy kept on loving his woman and camping outside her door until she could let him in." Louie's version was cleaned up a bit.

Louie and the band cut another six songs in New York City for Decca on October 14, 1939, all under the supervision of producer J. Mayo "Ink" Williams and with Stafford "Pazuza" Simon replacing Lem Johnson.

Showing his vocal versatility, Louie coos and sighs on Fats Waller and Andy Razaf's "Honeysuckle Rose" and then offers a bland blues vocal on "'Fore Day Blues." But he sounds in his element vocalizing the likes of "But I'll Be Back," "You're My Meat" and "You Ain't Nowhere"—funny pop songs with a jaunty tempo. While most of the material is average and the execution still an underdeveloped template, Louie and band give it all the spark they can muster.

Louie got writing credit on half the tunes and played alto sax, baritone sax and clarinet and sang. It was the beginning of a long relationship between Louie and Decca Records. His relationship with Ida would not be nearly as long-lived. But Ida, with her experience in the business and nurturing of his talent, was a driving force behind Louie during this period.

"Ida was ambitious for Louie," Courtney Williams, trumpeter in the early days of the Tympany Five, noted.

Chapter 4
"A GREAT TURNING POINT"

Louie's music matured rapidly as the 1940s progressed—even as the year 1940 progressed.

Soon, the fresh sound of Louis Jordan and the Tympany Five would dominate the American charts and provide the veritable soundtrack of the decade.

From the start, frequent rehearsals were the norm for the Tympany Five, just as they had been for Louie practically all of his life. As the leader, Louie maintained a distance from his players—cordial, of course, sometimes even quite friendly, but never really warm. As Louie's star rose, stories about his unbending ways as a bandleader would circulate—fines for missed notes, fines for unpolished shoes, fines for being late for the never-ending rehearsals. The tight, serious sound was in contrast to the loose, funny tone of the material.

On January 25, 1940, with J. Mayo Williams again producing, the band waxed Memphis, Tennessee native (and Louis Armstrong's ex-wife) Lil Armstrong's "You Run Your Mouth and I'll Run My Business"; "I'm Alabama Bound" (popular when Louie was born); "June Tenth Jamboree"; and "Hard Lovin' Blues," with Yack Taylor on vocals. Taylor's blues finds Louie answering Taylor's vocal lines with his own sumptuous clarinet lines.

Interestingly, "June Tenth Jamboree" has the same musical and lyrical opening as Louie and the band's song "Five Guys Named Moe"—"I want to tell you a story from way back, truck on down and dig me, jack"—which wouldn't be recorded for more than two and a half years. Beyond placing the setting in 1865, Louie doesn't give much of a history lesson about the

Written by "Kid" Wesley Wilson, 1940's "Do You Call That a Buddy?" was one of Louis Jordan's earliest Decca singles. Jordan would record other Wilson songs like "De Laff's on You," "Chicky-Mo, Craney-Crow" and "Somebody Done Hoodooed the Hoodoo Man."

Juneteenth celebration of the emancipation of African slaves in the United States, instead describing the gleeful swinging scene at a picnic ground, "mellow barbecue" and "fried chicken floating all around."

Adding clarinetist/tenor saxist Kenneth Hollon to the group, another half dozen sides were cut on March 13, 1940, in New York City with Williams. Like Yack Taylor in her guest vocal spot, Mabel Robinson handled vocals on the Jordan co-written "Lovie Joe," singing a great blues breakdown in the Bessie Smith/Ma Rainey style—albeit one that would have sounded dated in 1940. Daisy Winchester got a similar vocal turn on "You Got to Go When the Wagon Comes."

"Penthouse in the Basement" and "After School Swing Session (Swinging With Symphony Sid)" rounded out the session. Both tunes utilized the tympani drums, which were starting to prove unwieldy onstage and distracting on record.

New pianist Arnold Thomas (replacing Clarence Johnson), Walter Martin on drums, Courtney Williams on trumpet, Kenneth Hollon on clarinet and tenor sax and Charlie Drayton on bass composed the Tympany Five, but the lineup would soon evolve again.

By September 30, the Tympany Five's fourth Decca session of 1940, the band had crafted a good-selling side, "A Chicken Ain't Nothing but a Bird." Notably, this song first crystallizes many of the elements that would come to typify a Tympany Five song—humorous, hot rhymes and solid boogie over a shuffle beat, often on the lyrical topic of food. Chicken was a hit for historical figures like Caesar, the song explains, exploring various poultry preparation methods before concluding, "Chicken is still what you got."

• • • • • • • • • • • • • • • • • • •

"What I really tried to do, when I first got into music, I used to go into clubs and see guys come and sit there. The first thing they're into is what happened that day," Louie reflected in the early 1970s.

"I wanted to play music on stage that made people forget about what they did today. I always try to say something funny to corral their thoughts. That's my whole life."

By this time, a young assistant at the General Amusement Corporation booking agency named Berle Adams had noticed Louie's band. Adams tried to get them work and encouraged Louie to nurture and highlight his comedic talents. Adams would come to steer Louie's emerging career, as well as his own, through Louie's incredible rise through the 1940s.

They would both become rich. But right now, Louie was occupied with keeping his band together and his head above water. Bassist Henry Turner, who'd replaced Drayton, had left the fold, and Cave Springs, Missouri native Dallas Bartley filled the slot. A one-time bandleader and future solo recording artist himself, Bartley had played all around Chicago, including a transvestite club, where a song called "Five Guys Named Moe" brought down the house. Even better, Bartley's stage presence took some of the weight of showmanship from Jordan's shoulders. "Dallas Bartley was a godsend," Adams later said.

Louie continued refining his sound, retaining the Tympany Five name but dispensing with the eponymous tympanis, surely to drummer Martin's relief, since they were cumbersome, took up a lot of room onstage and were not used often.

With the United States' entry into World War II and resources like gasoline, metals and rubber becoming scarce, the Tympany Five's small size was all the more an asset. Beyond that, Louis Jordan and his Tympany Five would provide the musical backdrop, particularly for black America, through the wartime years. Louie would soon be recording topical material about rationing, WACs, war bonds and the like and doing benefits, special recordings and performances for the troops—on his way to becoming billed as the "Global Favorite of eleven million GIs."

Through 1941, Louie and the band continued recording in New York City with Williams for Decca. Louie stumbled upon a hit during the band's November 1941 sessions with its recording of a blues "I'm Gonna Move to the Outskirts of Town," coupled with a sexy number with plenty of food references, "Knock Me a Kiss," written by Mike Jackson. Both tunes would prove to be mainstays for the band, as would, to a lesser extent, Williams's "The Green Grass Grows All Around," sung in "round" style, and "Mama Mama Blues (Rusty Dusty Blues)."

The sessions were the recording debut of bassist Bartley and trumpeter Eddie Roane—and were the Tympany Five's first recordings in Chicago, as opposed to New York City, but still with producer "Ink" Williams. Pine Bluff, Arkansas–born bluesman Casey Bill Weldon had written "Outskirts of Town" and had a hit with it five years earlier. In Louie's hands, the blues song takes a more urbane turn musically and lyrically, and the humorous lament of a husband trying to keep his wife away from the charms of the ice man, grocery boy, et al, by moving away from the temptations of the city takes an even lighter form than Weldon's string band version. Louie's smooth vocal and general command of the song show a maturing artist and an artistic vision more fully formed.

• • • • • • • • • • • • • • • • • • • •

In 1942, another man with equal artistic confidence in himself and the performers he worked with would enter Louie's sphere as a producer, and the two would make musical history. Decca Records staff A&R man Milt Gabler, three years Louie's junior, would soon handle most of Louie's Decca sessions.

Together, they would make for some incredible record sales not to mention helping craft a musical shift in American culture. Gabler had been owner of the Commodore Record Shop in New York City. By the late 1930s, when Louie was doing his first solo recordings for Decca, Gabler had expanded from his record shop to doing recordings for his independent record label, Commodore, including the likes of Jelly Roll Morton, Billie Holiday and Teddy Wilson. In 1941, Gabler was advising Decca on what to re-release from the Vocalion-Brunswick catalogue, which it had acquired, and soon was offered a permanent position with the company.

Producing most of Louis Jordan's classic Decca sessions, Milt Gabler (seen at left in his Commodore Music Shop) was important to Jordan's sound. Gabler would go on to produce Bill Haley's similar-sounding "Rock Around the Clock." *Courtesy William P. Gottlieb/Ira and Leonore S. Gershwin Fund Collection, Music Division, Library of Congress.*

The stars of Louie, Fitzgerald and Gabler often intertwined but rose separately on Decca. With Gabler coming into the Tympany Five recording mix and Berle Adams continually promoting the group to white and black promoters alike across the country, all the pieces were coming together for Louis Jordan and the Tympany Five. Just in time for all this, Louie and the band completed a lengthy midwestern residency that brought the sound into sharper focus.

The Fox Head Tavern in Cedar Rapids, Iowa, was the unlikely venue where Jordan and the Tympany Five's fusion of musicianship and showmanship coalesced. "Now, it was just a beer joint," Louie remembered of the tavern. In hindsight, with its middle-America location and lack of extracurricular activities (especially for black musicians), it was perfect for Louie to hone the music that would appeal across demographics. The band was free to improvise, experiment with new material and clown, away from the scrutiny of their musician peers. Further, it was home to heretofore-untapped audience segments—the band hadn't played much for largely rural, white audiences. During the Tympany Five's residency there, the Fox

Head's owner let them rehearse at the club during the day. For once, band members welcomed rehearsals. Stage routines built around songs became almost as important as the songs themselves.

"The Fox Head in Cedar Rapids was a great turning point in my career," Louie would later recall. "It was there I found 'If It's Love You Want Baby, That's Me,' and a gang of blues—'Ration Blues,' 'Inflation Blues' and others."

When the band members completed the Fox Head residency in early 1942, they returned to New York City with plenty of new material, in both songs and stage business, as well as newfound confidence in their abilities and showmanship. Tellingly, the first song they attempted on July 21 when in the studio with Gabler for the first time was a straight-up novelty number, "What's the Use of Getting Sober (When You're Gonna Get Drunk Again)."

Just as tellingly, "Sober" became Louie's first number one hit.

It opens with a spoken-word intro with Louie as the "pappy"—who sounds pretty soused himself—admonishing his squeaky-voiced son to stop drinking so much, being concerned that the son's about to "blow his wig." But this morality tale is quickly forgotten as Louie begins rhapsodizing about various liquors he's loved since Prohibition was repealed. Recounting the previous evening's adventures in another spoken-word section, he keeps returning to get more booze on the hour and each time graduating upward from his initial half pint.

Louie had other songs on the radio and on jukeboxes and turntables. "Knock Me a Kiss"/"I'm Gonna Move to the Outskirts of Town" was doing well, as was "Rusty Dusty Blues"/"Small Town Boy."

Weldon's "Outskirts" did so well that an "answer song" was concocted and recorded: "I'm Gonna Leave You on the Outskirts of Town." The band also attempted another Casey Bill Weldon blues, "Somebody Done Changed the Lock On My Door," but didn't like the results. Three years later, Jordan would finally record and release a version of that Weldon song.

While "Small Town Boy" explored nostalgia lyrically, "Rusty Dusty Blues," also known as "Mama Mama Blues," hit on another recurring lyrical theme of Louis Jordan and his Tympany Five—that of conniving women. Although lighthearted on the surface, the undertones of "Rusty Dusty" are that of a prostitute who works her "big, fat rusty dusty" for the "bracelets and furs and Paris labels."

But the landmark Louie song recorded up to this point was "Five Guys Named Moe," cut at the same marathon session on July 21, 1942, that also yielded "Sober." The band had been playing "Five Guys" live onstage for some time, as is evidenced by the song's thundering pace, blistering solos and

Just a few years into a solo career, Louis Jordan was already a top name by the early 1940s; this advertisement is for a Little Rock concert. *Courtesy Stephanie Smittle.*

relentless rhyming on record. It was a showstopper live and lent itself well to the routines for which the Tympany Five were becoming known. From its opening line—"I want to tell you a story from way back / Truck on down and dig me, Jack"—"Five Guys" hooks the listener in with its bright rhymes and its "Moe-moe-moe-moe-moe-moe-moe" breakdown. The storyline of "the greatest band around" that is "the talk of rhythm town" doesn't really go anywhere but has a good time doing it.

Nine songs were cut at the session that day, more than half of which were useable. "De Laff's On You," an early calypso attempt, hit the cutting room floor, as did "Dirty Snake." Making the grade were "The Chicks I Pick Are Slender, Tender and Tall" and "That'll Just 'Bout Knock Me Out." Of the latter, Louie said, "That saying, 'That'll just about knock you out,' started from a white man in Grand Forks, North Dakota. The boss of the place had a husky voice; he'd say it all the time. That's where we wrote the song from."

It was a good thing the session turned out so well, for it was the only such recording session the band would do that year and most of the next, due to a recording ban instigated by the American Federation of Musicians over jukebox-play royalties.

Yes, just as things were heating up for them, Louie and his Tympany Five couldn't record. Louis found other ways to occupy himself during the ban. He'd reconnected with Fleecie Ernestine Moore, a childhood sweetheart from Brasfield, a small Prairie County, Arkansas town several miles southwest of Brinkley. Moore's family owned a restaurant in Brasfield and also farmed. They did well, and she became quite business-minded herself. Louie and Moore married in 1942.

Louie didn't mention Ida to Fleecie. Neither of them had heard about Julia.

Chapter 5
"STRADDLE THE FENCE"

Audiences in the northeast United States were discovering the power of Louie and his Tympany Five live following the tightening up that had occurred in Cedar Rapids. Most of the bands competing with Louie for bookings had four or five times the players, but Louie's Tympany Five was tearing things up in Chicago, Baltimore, Washington, D.C., Philadelphia and elsewhere.

"After my records started to sell," Louie said three decades later, "we drew mixed audiences to clubs like the Tick Tock in Boston, Billy Berg's Swing Club in Los Angeles, the Garrick in Chicago and the Top Hat in Toronto… That's how we did it in the early forties, so that we drew everybody. I was trying to do what they told me: straddle the fence."

The band's musical excellence and routines filled the stage where additional players might be. Louie and the well-rehearsed Tympany Five looked as tight as they sounded—all in sharp, pressed matching suits and syncopated stage moves. The conventional wisdom that a small band couldn't fill large concert halls—either musically or with crowds—had been turned around nearly single-handedly by Louie and his group.

In the space of less than two years, Louis Jordan and his Tympany Five had become one of the highest-paid and best-regarded live bands in the business. The band's hit songs were increasingly heard on radios, jukeboxes and Victrolas across the country. Louis Jordan was becoming a star.

Following a frightful notice to appear before his local draft board, he was rejected for military service due to hernia problems by early 1943. Louie

World War II helped popularize Louis Jordan's music internationally and make Jordan "the global favorite of eleven million GI's," as this Berle Adams Agency advertisement asserts.

would spend much time during the war entertaining Allied troops, but his draft deferment was much to the relief of the many people who were starting to make serious money on Louis Jordan and the Tympany Five—not to mention to Louie himself.

The phrase "Here Comes Mr. Jordan" began to appear in his promotional materials, as well as on Tympany Five bass drum fronts. It had been appropriated from a popular Hollywood movie of the same name starring Claude Rains and Robert Montgomery. (The film was remade in 1978 as *Heaven Can Wait*, starring Warren Beatty.)

An important song had come Louie's way as well. He added "Is You Is or Is You Ain't (My Baby)" to his set lists in the summer of 1943, and it rarely left them for the next three decades. The song begins with a dramatic descending piano figure under an equally ominous horn riff. "I got a gal who's always late," Louie intones, "any time we have a date…"

The tone brightens as the beat kicks in, and he reminds listeners and himself that he loves her and is going to ask her that musical question, "Is you is or is you ain't my baby?"

Louie and the Tympany Five recorded "Is You Is" that October. It was still new to the band when it was featured by Louie in the Hollywood movie *Follow the Boys*, also known as *Three Cheers for the Boys*. The film features a variety of performers, including W.C. Fields, Jeanette MacDonald and Orson Welles. Louie stars with George Raft in his scenes in the movie, wherein Louie agrees to play an impromptu set to entertain a segregated all-black regiment.

Offstage, Louie and Raft found they both shared fond memories of Hot Springs, Arkansas. Another song with Louie has Raft tap-dancing in the rain as the band plays "Sweet Georgia Brown."

(The front cover of the sheet music for "Is You Is or Is You Ain't" heavily promotes the song's appearance in the film but less so the performer of that song in the film. Louie's photo—showing him incongruously in his "Deacon Jones" stage glasses to boot—is at the bottom of the page. Despite Louie's obvious connections to the song in the film, his name on the sheet music front is listed below Raft, Zorina, the Andrews Sisters, Grace MacDonald and Dinah Shore, none of whom besides Raft even appear in the "Is You Is" scene.)

Louie's *Follow the Boys* cameo for Universal Pictures came after he was considered for another Universal project. It was described by its would-be producer, Lou Levy, as an all-black musical that would avoid the alleged Uncle Tom tendencies found in similar releases *Cabin in the Sky* and *Stormy*

This 1943 GAC advertisement shows some of the highlights of Louis Jordan's success, including top nightly concert grosses, millions in record sales and appearances in Soundies.

Weather. Both films were mainstream Hollywood movies that attempted to showcase black America more authentically than before—a low bar that neither reached. Unfortunately, the proposed film never came to fruition, but *Follow the Boys* no doubt helped raise the profile of "Is You Is or Is You Ain't (My Baby)," as well as that of Louie himself. At one point, Louie was topically dedicating the song onstage to actor Errol Flynn, who was in the midst of a paternity scandal.

"Is You Is or Is You Ain't" has been recorded by Frank Sinatra, Dinah Washington, Lionel Hampton and Nat King Cole, among many others. Some of Louie's duet partners on other songs have also tried their hands at the tune: Ella Fitzgerald, Bing Crosby and Louis Armstrong. Many others have recorded the song, such as the Andrews Sisters (who also appeared in *Follow the Boys*); Frankie Lymon and the Teenagers; Buster Brown; Glenn Miller; and, more recently, Diana Krall and B.B. King. Still another version of "Is You Is or Is You Ain't" underscores how widely popular the song was—one sung by Tom the cat in the 1946 Tom & Jerry cartoon *Solid Serenade*. "Is You Is or Is You Ain't" also became a number-one hit for Louie on the country charts for five weeks—another testament to the song's broad appeal. ("Is You Is" was one of Louie's two country chart toppers.) Louie continued recording versions of "Is You Is" throughout his career. That included on V-disc for the U.S. Armed Forces during World War II and in the 1950s, 1960s and up to his last solo recordings in France in late 1973.

• •

Louie would graduate from Hollywood cameos to starring in his own film vehicles, but next was Columbia's *Meet Miss Bobby Sox*, starring Bob Crosby. Louie squeezed in the film appearance during a month-long residency at Hollywood's Trocadero Club in May 1944. Louie and the Tympany Five—numbering only four here—perform "Deacon Jones." Decked out in thick, white-framed glasses; white shoes; a top hat; and a long coat with tails, Louie delivers different, even more scathing, lyrics than the Decca studio version recorded the previous autumn. He dances a flailing shuck-and-jive jig during the choruses that sends his coattails flying, while contrasting reaction shots show a sedate, seemingly uncomprehending audience of white teens. Despite the bobby soxers' rather mute reaction to the frantic antics, combine the outfit, glasses, dance and song, and it looks like Exhibit A for those who saw Louie as an Uncle Tom.

But any naysayers didn't seem to hurt his bookings. As *Billboard* reported in its July 22, 1944 issue: "Jordan is going through a double-date booking arrangement, playing for white and colored dancers for one-nighters in the Middle West. Leader recently played two dates in Oakland, California, where he drew 4,200 colored dancers at the Auditorium and 2,700 whites at Bill Sweet's the following night. Leader will start a one-nighter tour in September, playing for both sepias and whites in Kansas City, Tulsa, Oklahoma City, Chicago, New Orleans and Houston."

Louie and the Tympany Five also began starring in their own song-length "Soundies," early versions of music videos, which hit the scene in 1940. Soundies featured bands lip-synching their hits on 16-millimeter film screened on machines located in cafés and juke joints—like video jukeboxes. Production of the machines was soon complicated by World War II, but Soundies could be seen in hundreds of outlets across the country.

Louie's songs like "Five Guys Named Moe," "If You Can't Smile and Say Yes," "Old Man Mose," "Fuzzy Wuzzy," "Jumpin' at the Jubilee" and "Down, Down, Down" got the filmed Soundie treatment. The Tympany Five executed the moves and stage business they'd already sharpened on stage for the Soundie camera. Lip-synching was obviously still an emerging art at the time—as some band members amply demonstrate—but Louie generally pulled it all off with aplomb, and his on-camera magnetism is plain.

All the featured Soundie songs showcase Louie's mastery of rapid rhyming and novelty material—not only are there no ballads, but many of them have high-speed intricate wordplay. Although this particular aspect of Louie's music was emerging as his image, not all the Soundie songs saw release as singles on Decca Records.

Literally and figuratively, film magnified what Louie's audiences saw: a good-looking, consummate professional willing to do most anything to get over to audiences. He was a natural. The fans loved Louie on film. The feeling became mutual when Louie saw how the extra promotion boosted his concert attendance and record sales.

The same October 4, 1943 recording session in Los Angeles that produced "Is You Is or Is You Ain't (My Baby)" also saw eventual issuance of the topical war-related "Ration Blues" and "Deacon Jones," all co-written by Louie. Another song co-written by Louie, "The Things I Want I Can't Get at Home," was cut but stayed in the vault. "Deacon Jones" was a song that the band had built quite a routine around, with Louie wearing big glasses and playing the part of that ethically challenged man of the cloth, Deacon Jones, and featured in *Meet Miss Bobby Sox*. The song was adopted

Louis Jordan's 1944 number one song, "Mop! Mop!," tells what turned out to be a semi-autobiographical tale about a musician who finds "a riff that's new" and "still is making history."

from an old character from ribald minstrel and medicine show routines. It begins by noting that the song's "honored and respected" namesake won't be attending the day's services—he had a "slight accident." That plenty in the flock would have motivation to make Jones suffer an accident becomes plain, though its singer claims to praise, not bury, "handsome and good-looking" Jones. In a series of questions to which the answer is always "Deacon Jones," it is asked: Who takes the "chicken breast and leaves the giblets for the rest?" and when a sister of the flock is "all alone at night, who helps her see the light?"

The war was also providing good song material, and the commonality of the experience helped with crossover potential.

"Ration Blues" topped the R&B "Race Records" chart and was number one for three weeks on the country charts as well. For Louie, "the global favorite of eleven million GIs," songs like "Ration Blues" and "G.I. Jive" spoke directly to those experiencing the effects of war in civilian and military life, respectively. The narrator in "Ration Blues" notes the scarcity of sugar and meat and then uses the sexual double entendres to good effect. "You Can't Get That No More" was from the same March 15, 1944 Decca session with trumpeter Eddie Roane, pianist Arnold Thomas, drummer Wilmore "Slick" Jones and bassist Al Morgan (both formerly in the Fats Waller rhythm section) that brought forth "G.I. Jive," but it covers the rationing topic in a more literal manner than "Ration Blues."

"G.I. Jive," complete with its own Soundie, was written especially for Louie by noted songsmith Johnny Mercer. It hit number one on both the R&B and pop charts. Typical of Mercer, the lyrics were cutesy but clever and made good use of the acronym-driven U.S. Army: "If you're a P-V-T, your duty is to salute the L-I-E-U-T," the song explains, or face KP on the QT.

"Mop! Mop!," recorded at the same session, would also hit number one, and "mop" became part of Louie's lyrical vernacular. The song whimsically purports to tell the thousand-year-old story of Jungle Joe, a Zulu drummer who "made swing history." In hepcat patois, Louie describes how Joe is commissioned by the Zulu king to make "a riff that's new" or, the king warns, "your wig belongs to me." Ironically, the knee-knocking inspired by contemplating his own death supplies Joe with the beat that spares his life in "Mop! Mop!" Louie used the expression "mop!" to punctuate lyrics in other of his numbers like "Pettin' and Pokin.'"

In between these sessions was a March 1 recording session, the first of 1944, from which only "I Like 'Em Fat Like That" saw release. "How High Am I?," a love song to booze, "The Truth of the Matter" and "Hey Now Let's Live" were cut but not issued.

It was also the Tympany Five's first session with bassist Al Morgan. Born on August 19, 1908, in New Orleans, Louisiana, Morgan was a month younger than Louie. A player with Fats Waller, Coleman Hawkins and Cab Calloway—that's him on Calloway's classic "Minnie the Moocher"—Morgan came with a strong musical background that would have appealed to Louie. Morgan replaced Jesse "Po" Simpkins, who had been drafted by the U.S. Navy but would return to the band.

A September 1944 *Billboard* article noted the solidifying popularity of Louis Jordan and the Tympany Five, as it revealed the winners of a first-annual fan poll of the U.S. armed forces: "Louis Jordan pulls the surprise vote of the season with two sides in the Top 13, the only artist aside from Bing [Crosby] to get more than one record in the fave list."

Things were cooking for Louie professionally—and coming to a head on the homefront.

Berle Adams gamely sorts through the mess in his memoirs: "I was surprised by the news that Jordan was being sued for bigamy by his second wife, Ida," Adams says. "She charged that Louis married her while he was still married to Julie. Louie had told me that he'd married Julie in Brinkley and he had a child by that marriage…Because Jordan worked only weekends at the clubs, he was short on rations and salary. According to Ida, that's when she married Louis. She claimed she took in laundry and did other domestic work in order to sustain them. Louis argued his innocence by pointing out that Ida had been his and Julie's babysitter in Philadelphia, so she knew that he was already married."

Adams says he tried to get Louie to settle—"I told him that he was at fault, that he had married two women"— but Louie wouldn't hear of it. As he tells it, Adams went to Ida on his own and got her to agree to a $10,000 settlement, but Louie went through the roof when he caught wind. Louie put the brakes on the settlement proposal and stubbornly in effect sent the matter to public trial.

This 1944 songbook featured songs associated with Louis Jordan, like "Five Guys Named Moe" and "Knock Me a Kiss," but also several that aren't, like "Mister Freddie Blues," "See See Rider" and "Red Wagon." *Courtesy Old State House Museum.*

"The day before the trial began, I begged him to dress simply and play down his success," Adams writes. However, Louie "arrived in court expensively groomed, diamond ring and all. When I questioned him, he said, 'You forget, Berle, I'm a star. How do I explain a dour appearance to the news people?'"

Indeed, Louie liked to dress as sharply offstage as he required himself and his band to do onstage. He liked tailor-made suits and was especially fond of nice shoes. But perhaps due in part to his lack of sartorial discretion before the court, Ida won a $70,000 judgment. It was later reduced to $30,000 over three years, still plenty, Adams notes, "and Louis was in a high tax bracket." Not content with this portion of her ex's bubbling success, Ida began billing herself as "Mrs. Louis Jordan, Queen of the Blues, and her Orchestra," though Louie had that stopped.

In July 1944, Louie paired with Bing Crosby to record some duets, making it a meeting between the two hottest artists on Decca. The released results,

"Your Sox Don't Match" and "My Baby Said Yes (Yip, Yip De Hootie)," did well, though the material was hardly top-notch. In light of this and his previous successes, Louie was moved from Decca's Sepia series to the higher-priced Pop series—meaning more royalties. The stronger songs Louie and Crosby recorded at the session—Cole Porter's "Don't Fence Me In" and Louie's own "Is You Is or Is You Ain't (My Baby)"—weren't released, but Crosby had success later recording both of these songs.

The pairings of Louie with another Decca label mate, fellow east Arkansawyer Sister Rosetta Tharpe, have warranted less mention by fans of either performer. The two recorded together in January 1945 in Hollywood to give the troops a wartime boost with an Armed Forces Radio Service Jubilee radio broadcast. Louie and the Tympany Five played several such broadcasts. Though Tharpe has much stronger associations with Lucky Millinder and His Orchestra and did many such radio broadcasts with Millinder, Louie and Tharpe also performed some dates together.

It would be one of Louie's few direct connections performing gospel music; religious themes rarely entered the temple of the Tympany Five, save for the hilarious likes of "Deacon Jones." Still, the paths of Louie and Tharpe have several parallels: they were born within a few miles and within a few years of each other, both first recorded in the late 1930s for Decca and both rose to incredible fame in the 1940s doing a fresh take on an established musical style. Both spent the 1950s and 1960s with a lack of name recognition that belied their originality, and both died in the early 1970s in relative obscurity.

And years would pass before either's musical legacies began to be taken seriously.

· ·

Through the first half of 1945, Louie recorded such future Tympany Five stalwarts as "Buzz Me," "Salt Pork, West Virginia," "Don't Worry 'Bout That Mule," "Caldonia Boogie" and another Casey Bill Weldon blues, "Somebody Done Changed the Lock on My Door."

Three of the five—"Buzz Me," "Mule" and "Caldonia"—topped the *Billboard* "Race" (soon to be renamed "R&B") charts. So would his calypso duet that October with Ella Fitzgerald, "Stone Cold Dead in the Market."

"Buzz Me," number one for nine weeks, was another entry into Louie's bluesy-but-not-a-blues songs. After spending each verse telling his would-be lover to call him, he concludes each with "Come on over, you don't have to call at all." "Buzz Me" concludes with the ever-mortal line, "When I get my arms around you, ain't gonna let go until 1953!"

Surprisingly, "Salt Pork, West Virginia" is not an iconic Tympany Five food song but rather an iconic Tympany Five train song. The reveal at the end of the tune is that that's the singer's name for the city of Norfolk. It's not Louie at his cleverest, but the material is joyful and elevated by him and the band—and bolstered by the debut of electric guitarist Carl Hogan with a striking solo.

Number one for five weeks and written by Trinidadian Wilmoth Houdini, "Stone Cold Dead in the Market" showed that Louie and Ella Fitzgerald still had chemistry. With Caribbean accents, they tell a tale of marital violence, alternately concluding that the murdered was "nobody but her husband," and "he had it coming."

"Don't Worry 'Bout That Mule" only topped the chart for a week, but it survives as a rock 'n' roll prototype. It was featured in both the Louie film *Beware!* as well as in one of his musical cameos in *Swing Parade of 1946.* But none would catch fire in quite the manner as "Caldonia Boogie."

With things so hot for the Tympany Five, the chairs in the band were bound to get too warm for some members. By summer, "Wild" Bill Davis had replaced William Austin on piano, Eddie Byrd had replaced "Razz" Mitchell on drums, Jesse "Po" Simpkins had returned to replace Al Morgan on bass and Aaron Izenhall had taken over the trumpet chair that had been mostly held by Eddie Roane since the end of 1941.

Born in 1918 in Glasgow, Missouri, Wild Bill Davis wrote the Tympany Five's musical charts in addition to being the piano player. Davis recorded as a solo artist, toured with Duke Ellington and recorded with Johnny Hodges. Davis is credited with helping create the jazz organ sound, which he began during his tenure in the Tympany Five. Davis left the Tympany Five in 1947 but continued to supply Louie with band arrangements and, like many players, later rejoined the band. In June 1951, Louie and the Tympany Five cut Davis's song "Please Don't Leave Me," complete with Davis on vocals.

Tympany Five pianist William Austin isn't to be confused with songwriter Billy Austin. Born in Denver, Colorado, the latter Austin had a hand in such Louis Jordan and the Tympany Five numbers as "Is You Is or Is You Ain't (My Baby)," "Lay Something on the Bar (Besides Your Elbow)" and "Have You Got the Gumption?"

Louie had added an important new element to the Tympany Five sound—electric guitar. Guitarist Carl Hogan of St. Louis, Missouri, had joined the Tympany Five. Time would reveal both the choice to bring in guitar and to

Left: Look out, sister! Louis Jordan clowns around backstage while Tympany Five guitarist Carl Hogan (back left) and trumpeter Aaron Izenhall (back right) look dubious. *Courtesy William P. Gottlieb/Ira and Leonore S. Gershwin Fund Collection, Music Division, Library of Congress.*

Below: Louis Jordan and the Tympany Five in a promo photo for *Swing Parade of 1946*, an ensemble film also featuring Connee Boswell, Gale Storm and the Three Stooges.

have Hogan handle the duties to be fortuitous. The electric guitar was years away from becoming ubiquitous in American popular music, and it gave the Tympany Five a fresh sound. And Hogan and subsequent Tympany Five guitarists played a large, unheralded part in the electric guitar's popularity. There's Bill Jennings, James "Ham" Jackson, Bert Payne and Mickey Baker, but of all Tympany Five guitarists, Hogan is most often mentioned by other guitarists as an influence. Chuck Berry cites a section he took from Hogan's "Salt Pork, West Virginia" guitar solo to craft the "Chuck Berry riff." Hogan's "Salt Pork" solo is a fluid, single-string solo that is both jazzy and modern-sounding.

Louie and the band took a two-day break from their tour schedule at the end of July 1945 to shoot their part for the movie *Swing Parade of 1946*. Gale Storm received top billing. The musical acts, Louis Jordan & His Tympany Five and Will Osborne & His Orchestra, are billed at the bottom of the main acts. Mary Treen stars as Marie; she would soon begin production on the film *It's a Wonderful Life* as Cousin Tilly. The Three Stooges appear in their classic Moe, Larry and Curly incarnation, but *Swing Parade of 1946* is a forgotten part of Stooge lore, unmentioned even in Moe Howard's 1977 autobiography. In a tragedy of the comedic ages, Louie and the Stooges share no scenes together. *Swing Parade* is barely begun before Louie and the Tympany Five are shown performing their number-one hit, "Don't Worry 'Bout That Mule," while a nightclub is being renovated. Workers painting walls and sconces rock to the beat, as do a couple of adoring showgirls at Louie's feet.

On the swank nightclub's opening night, Osborne and orchestra get things moving with the floorshow and the film's title song. Connee Boswell sings "Stormy Weather," while Storm and company offer a song and extended dance number and partners in a romantic duet with co-star Phil Regan. The flimsy plot lurches on between songs until finally club headliners Louie and band return to the movie with their grandest entrance on film—on a darkened stage with their instruments outlined in neon to the orchestral strains of "Caldonia Boogie," re-recorded with strings and an additional outro section especially for the film. Louie puts down his neon-lined saxophone to join the dancers in a hoofing routine for the outro.

Then, Louie and the band aren't seen or mentioned again.

• • • • • • • • • • • • • • • • • • • •

"Caldonia Boogie" became one of the band's most enduring hits. The song, with its lyrical catchphrase, "Caldonia! Caldonia! What makes your big head so hard!?" set America on its ear. It spawned endless cover versions, two of which were released before Jordan's version hit the market.

Jordan's two film versions of the song—perhaps it could be said that *Swing Parade of 1946* was for white America and Louie's short *Caldonia* film was for black America—didn't hurt getting the word out on the song, either.

Louie first performed the song in 1944 for an armed forces Jubilee program. But the first recording issued was a revved-up version by Woody Herman and his Thundering Herd for Columbia in February 1945. It hit the pop charts on May 5, 1945. Erskine Hawkins followed with a version for RCA Victor that charted on May 12. Decca finally got the message and released Louie's version, which entered the charts in June. On the U.S. pop charts, Herman peaked at number two, Hawkins at number twelve and Jordan at number six. On the "Race Records" charts, Hawkins reached number two, while Jordan's original version hit number one and stayed on the charts for six months of 1945. Louie and other performers usually shortened the official song title to merely "Caldonia."

Following its success, many came forth to claim "Caldonia Boogie." Blues singer Sippie Wallace said the song was based on her song "Caldonia Blues" from the early 1920s. Louie acknowledged the lyric "Caldonia, what makes your big head so hard?" was lifted from a Hot Lips Page song. A lawsuit over ownership of the song would eventually go to the U.S. Supreme Court, but the song would remain Louie's—or, rather, wife Fleecie Moore's. Fleecie Moore was given writing and publishing credit for "Caldonia Boogie," as well as receiving co-credit for several other of Louie's important songs during their marriage, such as "Buzz Me," "Salt Pork, West Virginia," "Don't Worry 'Bout That Mule," "Let the Good Times Roll," "Beans and Cornbread," "Beware" and others, in a publishing and tax dodge gone awry.

Some twenty years later, when James Brown got the chance to meet Louie, Brown told Louie that he'd probably sung "Caldonia" as many times as Louie had. Brown recalled, "'Caldonia' was a song you could really put on a show with. And I guess that Louis Jordan short is what first started me thinking along those lines…I learned the words [to 'Caldonia'] as quick as I could, picked it out on piano and started playing it and singing it whenever I got the chance."

So did others. Benny Goodman, Memphis Slim, Carl Perkins, Muddy Waters, Roy Clark and Clifton Chenier are among the wide variety of giants in their own respective musical fields who've recorded "Caldonia Boogie." Young piano prodigy Frank "Sugar Chile" Robinson gives the song a workout in the 1946 film *No Leave, No Love* and had his own chart hit with it three years later.

Little Richard said "Caldonia Boogie" was the first non-gospel song he ever learned. That made sense, as Louie's "Cal-don-YAH!" shriek sounds eerily like the vocal tone Little Richard would adopt and patent to great chart success a decade later—as well as a Louie-style pencil-thin moustache.

The success of "Caldonia" spawned a film starring Louie and the band, which helped solidify his crossover appeal. The short movie was a big success. In 1946, *Billboard* magazine reported that the film was "one of the few all-negro productions to get bookings in white theaters." Headlined "Here Comes Mr. Jordan," an advertisement for the film proclaims Louie to be the "King of the Bobby Sock Brigade" and the "Global Favorite of eleven million GI Joes" while mentioning the film's attributes: "Solid with Jive," "Dancin'-Prancin' Sepia Beauties" and "4 Big Song Hits."

The ad shows Louie outfitted in his Deacon Jones attire of jacket with tails and white-framed glasses behind a pulpit with flames of hellfire drawn in below—although no such scene is in the movie.

Astor Pictures' *Caldonia* film short—the one that inspired a young James Brown—clocks in at under twenty minutes. It opens with Louie and the band performing in an upscale living room with a few show girls decorating the place, including Caldonia (Nicky O'Daniel), perched atop Bill Austin's piano swinging her long, lean and lanky gam in time. Bassist Al Morgan executes the looping iconic bass line with stars in his eyes. Trumpeter Eddie Roane and Alex "Razz" Mitchell line out the group, and Sam Theard, songwriter of "You Rascal You" and "Let the Good Times Roll," also appears as—who else?—his well-known nickname, "Spo-De-Ode-E." Would-be film producer Felix Paradise convinces Louie and the band to make films in Harlem rather than their scheduled Hollywood destination. A few overtures from Louie's comely gal Caldonia quickly convince Louie to stick around. But the lack of resources of the operation is the running joke: "I know, you've got number trouble—and the number is zero," Louie exasperatedly tells the producer.

Later, Paradise explains the repossession of the film company's camera with the plea, "So help me, Louie, when I saw the racing form this morning, what could I do?"

Louie convinces Caldonia to distract the repo man with her wiles as they finish shooting.

"Honey Chile" follows "Caldonia," and then comes a performance of the song "Tillie," which finds Louie and the band playing in the dregs of outlandish costumes hidden from repossession by creditors—clownish, mismatched outfits that the real Tympany Five would never wear onstage.

This ad for 1945's *Caldonia* features Louis Jordan in his "Deacon Jones" outfit for some reason. It being "the biggest extra added 'money' attraction in years" alludes to the film's crossover success.

Nicky "Caldonia" O'Daniel and Louis Jordan pose for a *Caldonia* publicity still. In 1946, *Billboard* reported that the film was "one of the few all-negro productions to get bookings in white theaters."

Still, Louie in full "Tillie" regalia—outsized bow tie, top hat and clashing long coat and striped pants—became the film's poster and an enduring image. In July 2008, the same *Caldonia* poster was featured on a United States Postal Service stamp recognizing U.S. black cinema.

Caldonia concludes with a performance of "Buzz Me." The song was the film's other big hit besides its namesake. Sheet music was produced for "Buzz Me," with the note on the cover that the song is featured in the Astor picture *Caldonia*. (Sheet music for the hit song "Caldonia" had already been issued.)

A final scene has the ostensible camera repo man "buzzing" Louie by phone while cozied up with Caldonia: "You can take care of that camera, but I'm the one who's going to take care of Caldonia," he chides an unseen Louie.

Chapter 6

"A NEW HIGH-WATER MARK"

Amid a decade of heights, 1946 was Louie's biggest year. In 1946, Louie had four of the year's five top songs on what was then called the "Race Records" chart. Two of these, "Ain't Nobody Here But Us Chickens" and "Choo Choo Ch'Boogie," spent an incredible combined thirty-five weeks at number one in 1946. That left only a scant seventeen weeks that year for someone other than Louis Jordan and his Tympany Five to be at number one.

Such sales make a future top-hitting Louie train song like 1947's "Texas & Pacific," number one for a mere two weeks, seem nearly trifling by comparison. Illustrating its broad appeal, "Choo Choo Ch'Boogie" has been recorded by bluesman B.B. King, zydeco great Clifton Chenier, western swing's Asleep at the Wheel and English blues rockers Foghat, among many others.

Many of Louie's biggest sellers—"Let the Good Times Roll," "Ain't Nobody Here But Us Chickens" and "Jack, You're Dead"—were released during this period. But Louie's biggest single ever was "Choo Choo Ch'Boogie," recorded in January. Milt Gabler, who had established himself as an important architect of the Tympany Five sound, brought the song to Jordan and received co-writing credit. The other writers were country and western performers Denver Darling and Vaughn Horton.

The song "Ain't Nobody Here But Us Chickens" became so popular that the song title became a slang catchphrase in America. So did other Jordan-related song titles "Open the Door, Richard" and "Let the Good Times Roll." (A friend of the author named Richard who grew up in the 1950s

The father of R&B in a familiar pose—putting his ever-changing Tympany Five through the paces. Note the faux piano keys at Louis Jordan's feet. *William P. Gottlieb/Ira and Leonore S. Gershwin Fund Collection, Music Division, Library of Congress.*

said he could never understand why adults were always telling him to open doors—until he finally heard the song.)

In another nod to Louie's ever-broadening popularity, Decca Records in 1946 issued a record album collection of four of Louie's 78s simply called *Louis Jordan and His Tympany Five.* The picture book–style layout of such collections gave us the term "album," still in use today. A smiling red-tinted Louie is featured on a bright yellow background on the front of the album; there is no back cover art, just exposed cardboard. The titles, in order, were

By 1946, Louis Jordan was popular enough to warrant his own "album," which was then a photo album–style collection of 78s bound in separate sleeves.

"Knock Me a Kiss," "I'm Gonna Move to the Outskirts of Town," "The Chicks I Pick Are Slender, Tender and Tall," "What's the Use of Getting Sober," "Is You Is or Is You Ain't," "Five Guys Named Moe," "It's a Low Down Dirty Shame" and "Mama Mama Blues." An advertisement for this Louis Jordan album collection quoted *Billboard* magazine, which said, "There should be extra dividends in this anew peddling." Like most Decca releases of the period, the individual record labels list the song's general feel—such as "Blues Dance," "Fox Trot," "Novelty Blues"—for the benefit of listener, dancer and disc jockey alike. With the newest of the included songs, "Is You Is or Is You Ain't," being more than two years old, the album was obviously meant not for casual listeners but for a burgeoning audience—the serious Louis Jordan fan.

Likewise, Louie's next film, *Beware!*, was upgraded from *Caldonia*'s tentative twenty minutes to a near hour in length and, by then, featured a revamped Tympany Five. Berle Adams had joined forces with R.M. Savini in producing the film. "Here comes that laughin,' lovin,' jumpin' and jivin' maestro with a beat," read the print advertisements for the movie, "starring in his first feature length, all colored fun packed musical screen show!"

Louie attended the premiere in Harlem, New York, following a Tympany Five gig at the Paramount Theater. Also in attendance at the movie premiere were Willie "The Lion" Smith, Pete Johnson and the Nicholas Brothers, as well as his former bandleader boss, Joe "Kaiser" Marshall.

The opening scenes of *Beware!* lack Louie but set up the plot: Ware College is losing money and enrollment under the reign of Benjamin Ware III (Milton Woods) and must close, as Ware III is cutting off the family endowment. A fundraiser is contemplated, since many Ware alumni have gone on to great heights in diverse fields. However, no one can imagine that a good end came to one student they happen to page by in a yearbook—shy and bashful Lucious Brokenshire Jordan, who was always bringing his saxophone to class. It is then revealed that Benjamin III's jealousy over Lucious and Annabelle Brown (Valerie Black), the comely alumnus-turned-faculty, caused Lucious to leave campus.

Cut to a great montage over Carl Hogan's opening descending guitar chords of "How Long Must I Wait for You?" featuring trains and B-roll of the actual Louis Jordan's sheet music, records, magazine covers, marquees and advertisements—much of it curiously promoting Louis Jordan and His Tympany *Six*—spliced in with train footage. The Ware top brass, stuck in their ivory tower, are out of touch with what's hip—Lucious Brokenshire Jordan is a huge star, though now known as "Louis Jordan." Lucious/Louie is rehearsing another train-oriented song, "How Long Must I Wait for You?," in his private car with his band. The train bumps to a halt. Louie gets off to call his manager Berle to tell him of the delay and laughs maniacally to learn he is in Ware, Ohio, home of Ware College. He gets the lowdown on Ware's woes from the white-haired professors.

Louie wakes the next morning in his old dorm room to wonderfully croon "Good Morning Heartache" while mooning over a photograph of lovely Miss Brown. In the classroom, "In the Land of the Buffalo Nickel" follows, with Louie delivering a would-be geography lesson to Ware students. The Tympany Five backs him—once again in a film, clad in uncharacteristically

The "laughin,' lovin,' jumpin' and jivin' maestro with a beat," Louis Jordan's 1946 full-length film, *Beware!*, came on the heels of the success of his *Caldonia* film short. *Courtesy Old State House Museum.*

ugly and clashing striped and checked sport coats, this time as a result of their layover in Ware. Louie then sings another brisk ballad, "Hold On," to keep up the spirits of the disappointed professors, who have received nothing but regrets from Ware alumni regarding a fundraiser.

Meanwhile, word has gotten around that the famed Louis Jordan is jamming at Ware; students are bopping to the sweet sounds of the Tympany Five as Louie and the professors rejoin the classroom to see the mêlée. "This is supposed to be the period for history," the professor gravely warns the dancing students, "and what you have been doing is far from historical!" Thus, Louie and the band launch into "You Got to Have the Beat." With its references to Christopher Columbus (the explorer, that is, not the future Tympany Five drummer), Paul Revere and Chopin *not* having the beat, this is obviously sufficiently historical. Oddly, none of these featured songs saw release by Decca.

Louie's back in a sharper, more typical suit for the next scene, with "Don't Worry 'Bout That Mule"—the film's first musical segment for an official

Decca release—prompted by Louie meeting the college mascot, which is, yes, a mule.

Following the song, Louie professes his love to Annabelle and learns from her that Benjamin Ware III is holding college funds hostage to coerce her into marrying him. A fundraising dance is planned, and Louie gets his personal accountant to come down and check the college's books. He finds irregularities committed by Ware the younger.

After Louie confronts Benjamin with the information and gives him a black eye off-screen, he gets Benjamin to announce at the dance that the college is back in good shape. The band then performs "Long-Legged Lizzie," with dancing by the perfectly cast Dimples Daniels as Lizzie.

After doing "Salt Pork, West Virginia," Louie publicly humiliates Ware further by dedicating "Beware" to him and singing every line to him. Following the performance of "Beware"—despite the fact that its anti-marriage lyrics aren't much of a slam on anyone but women—Benjamin storms off amid derisive laughter.

With things all reet at Ware College again, the guys are back on the train, jamming again, with Louie singing "An Old Fashioned Passion for You"—the only difference now being that Miss Brown has joined the entourage in Louie's train car, and the film ends with she and Louie's embrace and kiss as the song ends.

With the success of *Beware!* as both song and film vehicle, the title was capitalized on in some of Louie's press materials as well as in at least one of his endorsements: "Louis Jordan says 'Beware'—if you want to feel right, wear the best," reads one ad for tailor-made mail-order pants. "Louis says get yours from Hollywood Al."

A summer 1941 endorsement ad for Cleveland, Ohio's King band instruments dubs Louie "a modern artist" while still noting his past with the Chick Webb band. He's billed as "Louie Jordan" as opposed to "Louis Jordan" in the advertisement and pictured with a tenor sax as well as his more favored alto.

Louie's endorsement for U-Haul rental trailers billed him as a "favorite American entertainer and recording star." "A man who really moves around uses U-Haul rental trailers!" the headline of the ad reads, itself a nod to the migration of southern American blacks to the north and west for factory jobs and the hope for less strict enforcement of Jim Crow laws. Louie is quoted as saying the trailers can carry "everything from saxophones to steamer trunks."

Louie also endorsed Lander's Dixie Peach Hair Pomade—"makes hair smooth and lustrous"—and is pictured looking dapper in the ad head shot and named as "star of New York's famous '400 Club!'" In another hair-care advertisement, he is pictured alongside Sarah Vaughn, Count Basie, Dinah Washington, Isabelle Cooley and Erskine Hawkins endorsing Memphis-based Perma-Strate hair straightener: "These stars agree! It's always Perma-Strate hair straightener for natural looking straight hair that you can dress in any style!"

The July 8, 1946 issue of *Newsweek* magazine reviewed Louie's movie and came out on his birthday:

> *Last week, the Negro film industry reached a new high-water mark with the release of* Beware!, *an Astor Pictures production starring Louie Jordan, one of Decca's most lucrative recorders, Valerie Black, former leading lady of the stage hit* Anna Lucia, *and Milton Woods, the "colored Basil Rathbone." The picture cinches Jordan's reputation as a great melody maker but, catchy tunes aside, adds up to 55 minutes of heavy-handed melodrama inexpertly directed. The presence of Jordan, who has just made his third personal appearance at the Paramount Theater in New York, assures* Beware!'s *box-office success. The most successful Negro film to date was* Caldonia, *another Astor production with Jordan and his Tympany Five.*

With massive crossover success on the radio, in concert bookings, on the charts and in the movies, Louis Jordan's star was in full ascendancy.

Chapter 7

"YOU FOOL AROUND WITH THEM, YOU'RE GOING TO GET YOURSELF A SCHOOLIN'"

Louie had enjoyed a year of unprecedented popularity, incredible success and white-hot fame. But 1947 did not start out well.

Fleecie Ernestine Moore Jordan had learned of Louie's affair with Florence "Vicky" Hayes, which had been carrying on for more than a year. Even as road manager, Fleecie rarely went on the road with Louie, but she decided to join the group for its six-week residency at Billy Berg's Swing Club in Los Angeles, and they got an apartment in Pasadena. That Sunday, January 26, as the couple went to bed, the conversation became increasingly heated, and Fleecie's jealous rage reached a peak—and manifested itself in the form of a knife.

She stabbed Louie repeatedly, making connections to his face, his stomach and, as he tried to protect himself, his music-making hands.

He was taken to Huntington Memorial Hospital. Fleecie was arrested and charged with assault with a deadly weapon—the knife she had been using to trim corns from her feet.

Berle Adams recalled the story being the lead item on Walter Winchell's popular gossip radio program, which sprung Adams into action on the other side of the country. Adams called Billy Berg at his home for details; Berg wondered why Fleecie couldn't wait and stab Louie on Monday, when his Vine Street club was closed. Detroit, Michigan–born comedian/singer Timmie "Oh Yeah!" Rogers—author of Louie's "If You Can't Smile and Say Yes"—fronted the Tympany Five in Louie's absence.

With such violence happening toward the most popular black entertainer in the country, the story made an understandable splash, especially in the black press. The row made the front page of the *Chicago Defender*, which trumpeted "Louis Jordan Stabbed by Wife; Near Death" and in a smaller headline, "Mate, in Furious Rage, Resorts to Knife Slashing."

There was the very real possibility that Louie might lose the use of his fingers. Rumors spread that Louie had died.

"We had a quarrel when I came home from work. I got into bed and turned out the light. Next thing I knew I felt the knife go into my chest," Louie told a *Down Beat* reporter in the February 12, 1947 issue. "This is the second time Fleecie [has] cut me. There's not going to be another time."

The article noted the wounds Louie got from Fleecie's attack: "Jordan received several cuts on his hands and face and one gash missed his heart by about an inch. His left hand was cut badly...He also received a three-inch cut starting at the corner of his mouth and running diagonally downward."

The article continues: "Even Louis' daughter, in Chicago, had to call the Berle Adams office, Jordan's mentor, to find if reports about her dad [being dead] were true."

After Louie recovered, he declined to press charges of assault with a deadly weapon against Fleecie. Fleecie in turn dropped her charges of abuse against Louie. Still, the two readied for divorce, and both agreed to give Berle Adams power of attorney to divide their assets.

But—at least in his professional life—Louie wouldn't stay down long.

In March 1947, Louie received his first-ever gold record for "Choo Choo Ch'Boogie," while several of his other songs were quickly approaching the million sales mark. The attendant publicity photo of Louie, producer Milt Gabler and Decca vice-president Dave Kapp subsequently appeared in the April 12, 1947 *Billboard* magazine. "If all the copies of Jordan's best-seller and most-played disks were laid end to end they would probably make a shellac route across the country and back," the cover claims. "In the current *Billboard* lists, for instance, the Tympany Five titan has 'Ain't Nobody Here But Us Chickens,' 'Texas & Pacific,' 'Open the Door, Richard,' and 'Let the Good Times Roll,' riding high." It continues on, in the magazine's self-styled hepcat editorial voice, "Piloted by Berle Adams, the sax-tooted songsalesman [*sic*] has proved box office theaters and other personal appearance dates and his independently produced movie shorts are among the most solid grossers around the country for items of that type."

* *

He was indeed riding high. Louie's recordings during the first half of 1947 included such future Tympany Five standards as "Look Out," which was Louie's own answer song to his "Beware"; "Open the Door, Richard"; "Barnyard Boogie"; "Boogie Woogie Blue Plate"; and a pair of calypso numbers, "Early in the Morning" and "Run Joe," featuring the Calypso Boys on maracas and claves. "Boogie Woogie Blue Plate" would spend fourteen weeks at number one; "Run Joe" also topped the charts. The others became important Tympany Five songs.

"Open the Door, Richard" was recorded in January with the stone-solid Tympany Five lineup of trumpeter Aaron Izenhall, guitarist Carl Hogan, pianist "Wild" Bill Davis, bassist Jesse "Po" Simpkins, drummer Joe "Chris Columbus" Morris and James Wright on tenor sax. "Richard" was the band's adaptation of a musical comedy routine popularized by Clinton "Dusty" Fletcher and John "Spider Bruce" Mason, a version of which by tenor sax player Jack McVea was currently popular. Again portraying the drunken, self-deluding hipster, Louie talks his way through the song, singing only when the chorus comes around. Along the way, he drops one-liners like: "I'm going to drink to everybody's health until I ruin my own," "I know I ain't common, cause I got class I ain't never used yet" and "Imagine that old woman charging us three dollars a month, and getting mad 'cause we're twelve months in the arrears! Come meet me last Thursday saying, 'Ain't you boys going to give me some back rent?' I told her she'd be lucky if she got some front rent!"

William Forest Crouch, a director familiar to Louis Jordan fans, directed the promo film of "Dusty" Fletcher doing his "Open the Door, Richard" routine. And a film sequel with the song "Lazy Richard (Can't Get Him Up)" starred Stepin Fetchit and featured an uncredited Louie and the Tympany Five. Count Basie, the Three Flames and the Charioteers were among the other cover versions of "Open the Door, Richard" that came out around the same time.

"Look Out" employs a similar riff and the same talking-rhyme style used in "Beware." This time, the sage Louie is warning women of the untoward actions of the modern male. Over the cries of "stool pigeon," Louie gives the inside scoop on "some knowledge straight from the shelf—this is some jive I've used myself." But the inventive rhymes are still there: "If he says you look fetching, and wants to show you his etchings, don't go up there!," "If he says you look groovy, and he want to put you in a movie, he ain't no talent scout, and he don't know what it's all about!," "If he laughs at all your jokes, says he only drinks Cokes, your brand is all he smokes, and he want to meet your folks, don't believe him, it's a hoax!"

Conversely, "Beware" advised against predatory females "trying to hook you" in a variety of scenarios: "If nobody's looking, and she asks you to taste her cooking? Don't do it!," "If you go to a show, and she wants to sit in the back row? Bring her down front! Bring her right down front!," "If she calls you on the phone and she says, 'Darling, are you all alone?' No, you got three girls with you!" and the immortal "If her sister calls you brother, you better get further!" Both were hits.

Notably, while Fleecie Moore received co-writing credit for 1946's "Beware," as per Louie's unorthodox song copyright assignment method, the co-credit for mid-1947's "Look Out" re-write had reverted back to Jordan—reflecting the split with Fleecie.

It also reflected the untenable practice of giving lucrative, unearned songwriting credits in perpetuity to the partner of someone with Louie's marital track record. As they were duly assigned, Moore's heirs receive credit and royalties on key Tympany Five songs to this day. This includes "Beware," which sports many lines Louie must have found bitterly ironic in hindsight: "They ain't foolin,'—and if you fool around with them, you're gonna get yourself a schoolin.'"

With his fearless romanticism, there's little evidence Louie heeded his own advice to beware, brother, beware.

"Boogie Woogie Blue Plate" and "Run Joe" from the same April 1947 session (with Eddie Johnson now on tenor sax and Dallas Bartley returning to Tympany Five bass chores) likewise were each linguistically notable. The former's sung mainly in restaurant vernacular ("Comin' through with a slab o' moo"), and in the latter, Louie employs his patented faux Caribbean patois as he imparts the motley calypso tale of police-evading, fortunetelling scam artists.

Later, Decca issued an extended-play record release featuring Louie's songs "Caldonia," "Choo Choo Ch'Boogie," "Run Joe" and "Beware." The cardboard sleeve featured a black-and-white photograph taken at the April "Baby, It's Cold Outside" session that he and Ella Fitzgerald did that appeared on the cover of *Billboard* on May 28, 1949. Louie is pictured informally crooning in his suspenders and shirtsleeves, rather than in a suit jacket, with random papers in his breast pocket. This surely didn't please the always-dapper Louie.

The release was on a new format—45 rpm, which was smaller, thinner and less fragile than the 78 rpms that Decca and Louie had sold so extensively through the previous decade.

Meanwhile, as the Tympany Five turned, Joe "Chris Columbus" Morris had joined on drums and would stay in the Tympany Five through 1951 and

Jordan and the "Sweet Jordanettes" made the cover of *Color* magazine in August 1947.

still later return again to the band's drum stool in the 1960s. Josh Jackson, James Wright and Eddie Johnson would take turns in the tenor sax chair; it would revolve back to Jackson in 1949.

• • • • • • • • • • • • • • • • • • • •

Becoming a solid film attraction, Louie returned to the movie lot. In his 1947 film *Reet, Petite and Gone*, Louie again basically plays himself—a popular musician character with a name derived from his real name, this time as "Louis Jarvis." *Reet* opens with Jarvis and band finishing the chords to

"Caldonia" before doing a Tympany Five train song, "Texas & Pacific," live for radio broadcast. Representing Jarvis's band are Carl Hogan on guitar, Chris Columbus on drums, "Wild" Bill Davis on piano, James Wright on tenor sax and "Po" Simpkins on bass.

Of all of Louie's train songs, "Texas & Pacific" surely must be the trainiest. A spoken-word intro name-checks train lines across the country, from the Rock Island and New York Central to the Missouri Pacific, before launching into praise for the namesake train line of the song.

With the Tympany Five's signature shuffle beat so closely resembling the humming passenger trains of the era, it is little wonder Louis Jordan and his Tympany Five so often evoked trains.

After running through "All for the Love of Lil," the band is ready to launch into a (fictional) third number—"the new Louis Jarvis arrangement of 'Be Bah Bo Bip!'...the fastest instrumental you ever heard!"—when Louie suddenly gets word that his father is ailing and cuts the broadcast short, cueing the band to perform without him. Milton Woods, last seen as the notorious Benjamin Ware III in *Beware!*, now plays Louie's concerned (and more quietly lecherous) press agent Sam Adams.

The lineup of the Tympany Five had again changed since we last saw our celluloid heroes, but guitarist Carl Hogan remains and is as prominently featured as any of the band members—which is to say, very little.

Intriguingly, Louie also plays the young version of his father, Schyler Jarvis, distinguished in flashback sequences by a wider moustache and a bowler hat. He and Lovey Linn (Bea Griffith, also playing Honey Carter) sing "Tonight, Be Tender to Me."

Like some of the actual parallels to Louie's real life found in Louie's starring films *Beware!* and *Look Out Sister*, in *Reet, Petite and Gone*, Louie's film father Schyler Jarvis was an entertainer, like Louie's actual father, James Jordan. Louis Jarvis arrives too late to see his father alive.

While the elder Mr. Jarvis (J. Lewis Johnson) is on his deathbed working on some final, strange provisos in his will, others are scheming to nab his fortune. To inherit the estate, Schyler wants Louie to marry a girl with specific measurements within thirty days—measurements that, coincidentally, fit foxy Rusty (Vanita Smythe), one of the schemers, "to a 'T,'" as Louie notes. Upon having all this information, Louie wants nothing to do with Rusty, however foxy she may be, preferring to wait for true love. "You could learn to love me," she offers. "I can't afford the lesson!" he counters.

His manager, Sam Adams, advises that, considering Louie's upcoming planned show, they "sure could use some of that cabbage" offered in the will. Following "The Green Grass Grows All Around," Sam then announces that Louis Jarvis is casting the lead for his Broadway show: "We suggest that you come in your bathing suits," he notes, "to bring out the, uh, highlights."

June (June Richmond) and Honey Carter have been in a connecting subplot. They, too, arrived to New York City too late to see Schyler Jarvis alive, but Honey's mother knew the elder Mr. Jarvis and sang in his band, and Honey and June are looking for a break in showbiz. June then sings the ballad "I've Changed Completely," while Honey frolics nearby in her black bra and panties, enticingly rolling her stockings.

The need for music rehearsals of the Jarvis Broadway show provides the framework for "Wham Sam! (Dig Those Gams)" and the display of plenty of dancing and cheesecake leg footage as the casting call at Jarvis mansion gets underway.

"This is a number on how to understand women," Louie next informs the room full of women, telling them to pick up on it, by way of introducing "I Know What You're Puttin' Down." Adams, given the enviable task of taking the measurements of the hopefuls, also has to tell each lady that her measurements don't quite make it. (In a sly move, one girl is named "Helen Wheels.") But as the end of the casting call nears, no one has fit the exacting measurements. Honey comes in to audition at the last minute, and although she doesn't fit the measurements either, she gets reacquainted with Louis.

A Jarvis band rehearsal the next day gives the group an opportunity to work in "Let the Good Times Roll" in a backstage setting. This Louis Jordan number had a long gestation period, and although it never was a chart-topper, "Let the Good Times Roll" became an iconic Tympany Five song, later adopted by B.B. King, Ray Charles and others. Author Sam Theard had first shown the song to Louie in 1942. Louie refined "Let the Good Times Roll" on the road, claimed half writing credit (as Fleecie Moore) and recorded it in mid-1946. In the film's sequence of the song, the dancers' new costumes for the show are revealed—although unlike in the previous two film outings, the Tympany Five is never reduced to wearing anything other than their typically sharp matching suits.

"Wham, Sam, dig those gams," Louie says to Sam in admiration of the ladies. The band then launches into the film's namesake, "Reet, Petite and Gone." June gets the chance to sing in the rehearsal; though her wide frame assures she isn't in contention for the measurements of the lead, she is given a singing contract by Jarvis.

But meanwhile, Schyler's lawyer and Rusty have managed to give the investors in Louie's Broadway show cold feet in hopes of getting Louie to marry Rusty. Louie is on to them and tells them so, but it still appears that Louie's Broadway show will close before it even opens. However, it turns out the evil lawyer had the will changed to fit Rusty's measurements—when Schyler, somehow, originally had them specific to those of Honey Carter, the daughter of his true, unrequited love.

The Louis Jarvis Broadway show, named *Swing Out Loud* and shown in a marquee shot, completes the film's third act. The Jarvis show's featured tunes—a tepid barnyard/food/double entendre formula piece, "That Chick's Too Young to Fry"; a Jordan-as–Fleecie Moore co-written boogie, "Ain't That Just Like a Woman"; and "If It's Love You Want, Baby, That's Me," with plenty of posing sepia beauties filling out the frame—finish out Louie's second full-length film vehicle. (Carl Hogan's "Ain't That Just Like a Woman" intro is also an acknowledged portion of Chuck Berry's well-known riff. The song has been covered by Berry, Fats Domino, "Gatemouth" Brown and B.B. King, as well as less likely suspect Alice Cooper. Jordan's version is also on the *Mafia II* video game soundtrack.)

As 1947 drew to a close, Louie and the band recorded several sessions for Decca in Los Angeles, in advance of another recording ban stemming from differences between recording companies and the musicians' union. He and the band wouldn't have another official Decca recording session again until February 1949.

It's worth noting that for all the record sales and chart success that Louie enjoyed through the 1940s, he and the band were unable to record for more than two years of that time due to recording bans. A full two years is also about the amount of time during the decade that a Louis Jordan song topped the charts.

Releases from the sessions included another song told from the point of view of a partier "higher than a fly on the spray" asking a law officer, "'Have You Got the Gumption' to make the assumption that I'm inebriated?"

Other notables from the late November–early December sessions include "You're Much Too Fat (And That's That)," "Pettin' and Pokin'" and the mellow blues "We Can't Agree." B.B. King covered the latter, which includes such priceless lines as "You're used to eating hot dogs whenever you go out to dine, I taught you what a steak was, now you suddenly lost your mind."

By contrast, the Jordan-written "Pettin' and Pokin'" is another rapid-fire rhyme fest, with Louie rapping about the volatile couple next door, who are "always pettin' and pokin,' and jabbin' and jokin,' and cooin' and crackin' and wooin' and whackin'—they keep neckin' and knockin' and singin' and sockin,' squawkin' and squeezin' and burnin' and freezin'…"

"You're Much Too Fat (And That's That)" contradicts the sentiment of 1944's "I Like 'Em Fat Like That" but nicely dovetails with 1942's "The Chicks I Pick Are Slender, Tender and Tall." As with "Beware" and its answer song, "Look Out," Louie was willing to play both sides of the fence.

A beautifully sung Jordan-written ballad cut at the December 1, 1947 Los Angeles session, "There'll Be No Days Like That," wasn't released, but a lesser song with a similar feel, "Why'd You Do It, Baby," did see single release.

Another release was the pair of playfully combative duets that Louie and Martha Davis recorded with the band a week later: "You're On the Right Track, Baby" and Don Raye and Gene de Paul's "Daddy O." The record label of the latter song notes that "Daddy-O" is from "the Samuel Goldwyn production *A Song Is Born.*"

Then, Louie took a rare break.

During the lull, Eddie Johnson, Carl Hogan and Dallas Bartley left the Tympany Five, a unit that had remained quite fluid despite the band's steady concert, chart and film successes. Louie and Fleecie Moore attempted another reconciliation and returned to east Arkansas to visit their respective families and in-laws.

Also during the break, Louie had plastic surgery on the facial scars that Moore had given him during the stabbing attack, and he recuperated in Florida.

"Jordan Makes Florida History," proclaimed a headline over a photo in the December 3, 1947 issue of *Down Beat* magazine. Louie is pictured on Coral Gables, Florida radio station WBAY's *Record Collector* program. According to the radio program's host, Walt Lyndon, "this marks the first time any Negro artist has ever appeared as a guest star on an established program in Florida." The article noted that the station is the only one in the South carrying "colored and white advertisers equally and mixed during its broadcast time."

But soon, Louie was back cracking the whip, rehearing his new version of the Tympany Five. The band had plenty of bookings to complete in 1948. One at the end of the year merited reportage in the December 15, 1948 issue of *Down Beat* magazine: "Jordan Doesn't Like It, but He Plays, Anyhow," the headline read. The November 22 concert at the New Orleans auditorium segregated black patrons in the balcony, with the main floor open only to whites—"who hardly showed up anyway," the article noted.

"If I'd known that Negroes would not be allowed to sit downstairs, I'd have canceled the show," Louie said. "I don't stand for that sort of thing, and

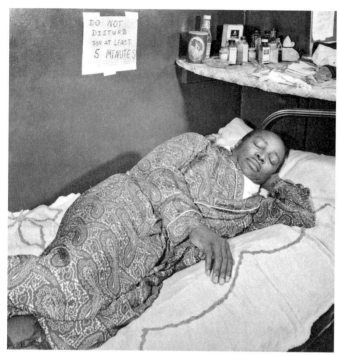

Left: Always dapper, even in repose, Louis Jordan catches a few winks backstage. *William P. Gottlieb/Ira and Leonore S. Gershwin Fund Collection, Music Division, Library of Congress.*

Below: "Two Gun" Louis Jordan's 1947 full-length film vehicle, *Look Out Sister*, was a western. *Courtesy Old State House Museum.*

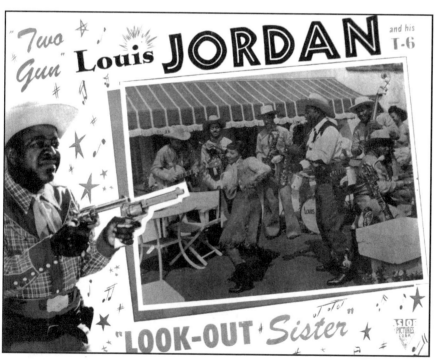

I don't need the money. I'm going to play, but I won't like it." Only 3,850 turned out for the 8,200 seats. Louie opened the show with his 1942 song "It's a Low Down Dirty Shame."

Louie spent 1948 touring instead of recording due to the ban. With he and the band still so hot, it was a too-long respite. But there were other ways to keep the Louis Jordan and Tympany Five name out there, such as the new movie vehicle *Look Out Sister*, Louie's third and final full-length film.

Look Out Sister is of particular interest to fans in that some musical segments appear to be actually performed live, and several scenes were filmed at Louie's real-life home in Phoenix, Arizona. Again, the film is an Astor Pictures film, though this time, only R.M. Savini "Presents" the picture, with Berle Adams listed as producer.

Somehow, in Louie's own starring vehicle, the Tympany Five band name is misspelled, and misnamed, as the "Tympanny Band" in the film credits. James "Ham" Jackson had replaced Carl Hogan on electric guitar, with Aaron Izenhall on trumpet; Bill Doggett on piano; Chris Columbus on drums; Paul Quinichette, who had replaced Eddie Johnson, on tenor sax; and Bill Hadnott on bass, replacing Dallas Bartley.

The often-transitory nature of being a member of the Tympany Five, however, is revealed through the early course of *Look Out Sister*—a different version of the band is on board for the opener, "Jack, You're Dead," than for the rest of the film. Trumpeter Aaron Izenhall provides the only band continuity. With the identical recording studio set as "The Green Grass Grows All Around," previously seen in *Reet, Petite and Gone*, "Jack, You're Dead" appears to have been shot independently of the *Look Out Sister* film as its own Soundie.

The train/Tympany Five montage with the opening chords of "How Long Must I Wait for You?"—already seen in the film *Beware!*—is re-used for the opening of *Look Out Sister* but quickly segues into the band playing "Jack, You're Dead," a chart-topper for seven weeks, in the studio.

The film features several songs that he and the band recorded for Decca in 1947—"Look Out," of course, plus "Don't Burn the Candle at Both Ends," "We Can't Agree," "Roamin' Blues," "Chicky-Mo, Craney-Crow," "Barnyard Boogie" and "You're Much Too Fat (And That's That)."

Another segment of the now thrice-screened montage—used, conversely, here to illustrate the pressures facing in-demand, ever-grappling bands like the Tympany Five—comes before a fast, seemingly live version of "Caldonia Boogie," with Louie limping off, mid-song, apparently in pain.

Diagnosed with "overwork" and placed in the Park View Sanatorium, he is befriended by Billy (Glen Allen), a cowboy-loving sick kid who can't understand how a big star like Louie doesn't know how to ride or rope.

In *Look Out Sister*, like the other films, Louie's manager is mentioned, though never seen, and here is named "Dick Adams." Adams is the recipient of a phone call from irate club owner Mark Morgan, who is afraid Louie's hospitalization will affect the booking he has with Louie. "If Jordan would stop playing so many benefits, he wouldn't have a breakdown," Morgan (Monte Hawley) snarls into the phone. Appropriately, Hawley also plays the heavy in Louie's cowboy dream sequence that composes most of the film.

After taking medicine from Nurse Betty (Suzette Harbin), Louie begins dreaming of a place for sick children to enjoy the great outdoors while convalescing. With the setting now in Lookout, Arizona, we see Louie, the band and others in an open stagecoach as he sings "My New Ten-Gallon Hat." The group is on its way to the H&H Ranch ("Health and happiness, two wonderful words," Jordan notes). Here in Lookout, Louie is known as "Two-Gun Jordan."

The conflict in *Look Out Sister* features a classic Hollywood western trope: bad guys knowing there's oil beneath the land and trying to get the deed by causing trouble. "Lady, you got me wrong—I don't ride 'em, I play 'em!," Louie exhorts of horses to Harbin early on, though his real-life horse riding lessons back when he lived in Hot Springs helped out during the filming.

After learning of H&H's financial woes, Louie says he and the band are having such a good time at the ranch, they're glad to stay on and play for free. Informed of bad-guy chicanery concerning the mortgage, he additionally offers to "wire all the stars of stage, screen and radio, and we'll fix up everything."

Meanwhile, back at the ranch, the Jivin' Cowhands perform the instrumental "Turkey in the Straw" as Louie and Peggy Thomas square dance. Louie then rejoins the band to sing "Roamin' Blues" and a funky "Early in the Morning."

(Peggy Hart Thomas gets low billing in *Look Out Sister* as "Dancer," appearing in the credits just above Louise "Bathing Beauty" Franklin and "Girl Exhibition Divers" Anice Clark and Dorothy Seamans—especially considering she had been dancing with the band since 1944 and would continue to do so off and on for some years to come. Her romance with Tympany Five tenor sax player Paul Quinichette contributed to his firing from the band and Louie bringing back Josh Jackson to the fold. Thomas accompanied the band on their tour of the Caribbean in March 1951. She left the group that summer to join pianist Erroll Garner as his companion on the road.)

The band plays the title song, "Look Out Sister," as the horse-thieving conspiracy boils to a head, based solely on the "evidence" of Louie's planted bolo tie. The crowd, which had just been in the palm of his hand, quickly turns ugly.

"You're nothing but a common horse thief! And we thought you were such a great man, Mr. Two-Gun Jordan," snaps Harbin, who has turned from pretty nurse into pretty ranch hand in Louie's dream—and just as quickly turns on our hero. When the frame-up is just as quickly exposed, a chair-smashing brawl ensues. Louie executes some funny Popeye-style pugilistic maneuvers during the mêlée, but his gingerly smashing the breakaway chairs on foes is inadvertently comic. A lengthy chase and shootout follows, scored with an instrumental rave-up of "Let the Good Times Roll."

Louie, awakened from his fever dream still holding the imaginary reins from the chase, resolves to open up a ranch in Lookout for sick children and makes a call to set it up. Louie's sexy Nurse Betty overhears and gives him a big kiss for his generosity. As Louie goes back for seconds, little Billy exclaims, "Look out, sister, look out," and shakes his head ruefully at the impertinent adults.

• • • • • • • • • • • • • • • • • • •

Louie's screen presence was obvious. And despite his talents as a singer of ballads and horn player, Louie remains best known, then and now, for his uptempo near-novelty songs like "Caldonia Boogie," "Ain't Nobody Here But Us Chickens," "Choo Choo Ch'Boogie," "Five Guys Named Moe" and "Saturday Night Fish Fry." But yet another overlooked wrinkle in the talent and influence of Jordan is his embrace and popularization of calypso music.

In April 1947, Jordan recorded two important calypso songs: "Early in the Morning" and "Run Joe." Over the funky piano riffing of "Morning," Louie demonstrates his talent to infuse blues overtones into material without ever crossing the line to make it straight blues. Even the song refrain speaks to this, with the line "It's early in the morning, and I ain't got nothing but the blues."

By contrast, "Run Joe" is taken at a quicker pace. Like so many calypso songs of this era, it tells a morality tale of miscreants or law-breakers getting their comeuppance—also a theme in similar Tympany Five calypso numbers as "Stone Cold Dead in the Market."

It was a decade before the American calypso boom, but Louie had long been interested in the music. He'd tried to accommodate bandstand requests from island immigrants who came to the clubs he played in the American Northeast and South.

Since she started with Louie and the band in 1944 as a singer and dancer, Peggy Thomas had taught him songs from her youth in Trinidad. His physician solidified Louie's decision to regularly feature Caribbean music in his sets. Dr. Walter Merrick was born in 1896 on St. Vincent and became a composer and historian of Caribbean music. Merrick co-wrote "Run Joe" with his Trinidad-born lyricist, Joe Willoughby. *Jet* magazine reported that Merrick was writing a calypso musical that would feature Jordan, but it didn't get off the ground. Jordan co-wrote "Early in the Morning," and in April 1952, he recorded a song he'd co-written with Willoughby called "Time Marches On."

Just as notably, the impact of the music of the Tympany Five rippled to other islands in the region, influencing reggae, ska and rocksteady—indigenous sounds that would in turn hop the border and come to be appreciated worldwide.

Jamaican singer Alton Ellis, known as the "Godfather of Rocksteady," said, "The ska came from American music. We used to dance to that music, because [influential ska and reggae producer Clement 'Sir] Coxsone' [Dodd] used to buy rhythm and blues music from America…songs by people like Louis Jordan."

Louis Jordan and the Tympany Five finally returned to the studio in February 1949.

Given his tumultuous marital situations, 1949's "Safe, Sane and Single" must have appealed to Louie, even if he could not heed the advice. The song is done in a hokey style at a rapid clip, with the quick wordplay attempting to mask the inherent corniness of lines like, "If my horse could only cook, I'd marry him instead."

"I Know What I've Got, Don't Know What I'm Getting" was by Sid Robin, writer of Louie's "If It's Love You Want Baby, That's Me" and co-author of "Look Out" and Louie's duet with Bing Crosby, "My Baby Said Yes (Yip, Yip De Hootie)."

The February 7 session in Los Angeles saw Bill Doggett replacing "Wild" Bill Davis on piano and Billy Hadnott replacing Dallas Bartley on bass. It was also Louie's last recordings with guitarist Carl Hogan. Hogan had been with the Tympany Five for nearly five trend-setting years. James "Ham" Jackson replaced Hogan on electric guitar—with the electric guitar now unquestionably tied to the Tympany Five sound. And, despite the recording break, don't think Chuck Berry and countless others weren't noticing that sound.

Beware, brother! Surrounded by his Jordanettes backstage, Louis Jordan obligingly surrenders his alto sax for the photo op. *William P. Gottlieb/Ira and Leonore S. Gershwin Fund Collection, Music Division, Library of Congress.*

A newspaper article promoting a Labor Day (likely 1948) personal appearance by Louie at Peacock Recording Co. in Houston, Texas, lays out Louie's successes: "His total record sales are in the neighborhood of twenty million, a mark that few others can even approach. Today, Louis Jordan is the number one Sepian attraction on Decca. His initial pressings vary from fifty to one hundred thousand platters, depending on the song. There are less than ten artists in the world who get that kind of minimum sales."

The band did three New York City Decca sessions with Milt Gabler in April, including "Onion" and "Psycho-Loco," a pair of instrumentals co-written with keyboardist Bill Doggett, the latter hinting at the new hip strain of jazz called bebop.

To a younger generation of listeners, bebop *was* jazz. "Like bebop? Man, I love it. That's for me," Louie said in the March 10, 1948 *Down Beat*. "You know Dizzy Gillespie's my boy. I worked with him back when I was with Chick Webb and he was with Teddy Hill at the Savoy Ballroom. That was when Dizzy was first starting. We've got seven or eight bebop numbers in the book right now," he claimed, "but you can't put them over on the stage. Not now. Maybe in a couple of years when people get educated to it. We play them at dances now."

In reality, bebop was anathema to Louie's musical aesthetic, and the revolution it created in jazz would leave him dismissed in jazz circles. With rhythms and riffs that are purposefully challenging to musicians and listeners alike, bebop was music for musicians—the polar opposite of the Tympany Five.

That month, Louie and the group also recorded the food- and Arkansas-themed "Coleslaw," the calypso "Push-Ka-Pee-She Pie (The Saga of Saga Boy)" and "School Days," which became a solid hit.

The band finally got a satisfactory take on "Beans and Cornbread" after unissued attempts at the song two years before. "Beans and Cornbread" became another number-one song for Louie.

With cohort Milt Gabler, Louie and Ella Fitzgerald teamed up to record a pair of duets on April 28: "Baby, It's Cold Outside" and "Don't Cry, Cry Baby." A publicity photo of the pair singing in the studio made the May 28, 1949 *Billboard* cover. Frank Loesser's "Baby, It's Cold Outside" would eventually evolve into a holiday favorite, and the song title became a catchphrase.

A radio transcription of an April 1949 gig from Los Angeles's Hollywood Empire reveals a typical Tympany Five set of the era with Aaron Izenhall, Bill Jennings, Bob Bushnell, Joe Morris and Bill Doggett. The newly recorded

"Safe, Sane and Single" commingles with emerging warhorses "Choo Choo Ch'Boogie," "Let the Good Times Roll," "Buzz Me," "Knock Me a Kiss," "Is You Is" and a particularly hot "Five Guys Named Moe." Bixie Crawford sings Martha Davis's part in a faster, still-new "Daddy-O."

In August 1949, Louie and the Tympany Five recorded a pair of Bobby Troup songs, "Hungry Man" and "Love You Til Your Money's Gone Blues," which wasn't issued.

More importantly, they cut "Saturday Night Fish Fry," credited to Louie and Ellis Walsh. Featuring two additional trumpeters beefing up Aaron Izenhall's horn, it became the band's top food song. The tune also spanned both sides of the 78 rpm single; the long story-song had to be divided in two to complete the tale. "Fish Fry" was number one on the R&B charts for twelve weeks total.

With World War II and America's "Second Great Migration" to points north and west for defense jobs in full swing, Louis Jordan endorsed U-Haul.

Saturday Night Fish Fry

By ELLIS WALSH and LOUIS JORDAN

Recorded by LOUIS JORDAN on Decca Record No. 24725

Preview-Music COMPANY
6419 Homewood Ave., Hollywood 28. Cali

Often cited as being among the first rock 'n' roll records, Louis Jordan's 1949 number-one R&B hit "Saturday Night Fish Fry" warranted its own sheet music. The long song took up both sides of the 78 single. *Courtesy Old State House Museum.*

"Saturday Night Fish Fry" is often cited as being among the first rock 'n' roll records. But if beat is the qualifier, Louie had been doing rock records for some time, as his acolytes later allowed—and the opening of Louie's "Don't Worry 'Bout That Mule" from 1945 is similar to the cadence of the quintessential early rock song "Blue Suede Shoes" a decade later.

At least some of the historical credence given "Saturday Night Fish Fry" seems to stem from the chorus: "It was rockin.'" But, like the often-unaccredited rocking Louie was doing in the pre-rock era, there had been American songs glorifying "rocking"—generally as a euphemism for sex—for years prior to the advent of rock 'n' roll.

Chapter 8
"A PERFECT SHOWMAN"

Time brought more changes to the Tympany Five: Billy Hadnott had replaced Dallas Bartley on bass, Hadnott had been replaced by Bob Bushnell and Bill Jennings had replaced James "Ham" Jackson on electric guitar. Previously a Tympany Five pianist, "Wild" Bill Davis rejoined the band to add a modern element—electric organ. He'd originally left the group in part to learn the expensive new instrument.

With the piano services of Bill Doggett still being retained in the Tympany Five, "Tamburitza Boogie" and "Lemonade," co-written by Louie, featured Davis. Recorded at the same August 18, 1950 session were "(You Dyed Your Hair) Chartreuse," "It's a Great, Great Pleasure" and "You Will Always Have a Friend." The latter two were co-written by Louie with old collaborators, New Orleans–born William Tennyson and Trinidad-born Joe Willoughby, respectively, but lacked the spark of the likes of their "Salt Pork, West Virginia" and "Run Joe."

The August 11, 1950 *Down Beat* told of bigger changes in Louie's world: "Berle Adams, personal manager of Jerry Gray and Louis Jordan, has dropped out of the personal management field to join the Music Corporation of America where he will concentrate on building new talent."

Also in August 1950, Louie and the band, with Ella Fitzgerald, cut "Ain't Nobody's Business But My Own" and the gorgeous ballad "I'll Never Be Free."

Louie and Ella would never record together again.

It was a busy month of Decca recording sessions. A little more than a week after he and the band recorded with Fitzgerald, they recorded a pair

One of Louis Jordan and Ella Fitzgerald's duets, "I'll Never Be Free," hit the R&B top ten in 1950. Jordan remains an underrated vocalist, particularly in his balladry.

of duets with another musical great from his past who had come a long way—Louis Armstrong. Louie and Louis cut "Life Is So Peculiar" and the Armstrong chestnut "I'll Be Glad When You're Dead (You, Rascal, You)," written by Sam "Spo-Dee-O-Dee" Theard, co-author with "Fleecie Moore" of Louie's signature tune, "Let the Good Times Roll," and of 1944's "You Can't Get That No More."

After explaining that hours were spent with Armstrong nursing hoarseness and a busted lip, Louie recalled to Steve Allen in 1973 about the Satchmo session, "We started the session about 10:30 or 10:45 and we were through in ten minutes. We had talked it over and he'd looked at the music and we knew what we were going to do, but we had to wait on his lip. Finally, he says, 'Let's go,' and we went and played it. He even played those high Cs and things with his lip busted. He was magnificent."

However, Bill Doggett told WKCR radio in 1991 that, in reality, all-business Louie was "fit to be tied" about the lack of punctuality at the session.

Louie and Louis also would never record together again.

By December, when Louie returned to Decca studios, Bill Doggett had left to pursue his own electric organ solo dreams. They cut "Teardrops from My Eyes" and "If You've Got Someplace to Go." Only "Teardrops" was released, while the brooding "If You've Got Someplace to Go" is one of the darkest songs in Louie's canon. "If you've got someplace to go, go ahead," Louie somberly sings over Davis's swelling, soap-opera organ intro, "'cause as far as I'm concerned, you're dead."

That June, Louie and the Tympany Five recorded "Blue Light Boogie," a two-sided "part one and part two" disc written by female Texas writer Jessie Mae Robinson. Like so many of Louie's best-known songs, the setting in "Blue Light" is a party. But the key difference here—perhaps tellingly—is that the narrator is unable to boogie like the others at the party: "I started swinging, all she did was rock." By the song's end, he laments that he "was like a chaperone." With outstanding soloing from Bill Jennings on guitar and Bill Doggett on piano, "Blue Light Boogie" topped the charts for seven weeks.

It would be Louie's last big number-one hit.

• • • • • • • • • • • • • • • • • • • •

On March 1, 1951, with producer Milt Gabler, trumpeter Aaron Izenhall, tenor saxist Josh Jackson, bassist Bob Bushnell, drummer Joe "Chris Columbus" Morris, pianist "Wild" Bill Davis and guitarist Bill Jennings, Louie cut "Is My Pop in There?," "I Can't Give You Anything But Love, Baby" and his own composition, "Weak Minded Blues," in New York City for Decca.

"I Can't Give You Anything But Love, Baby" and "Is My Pop in There?" feature a group vocal, like previous Tympany Five songs "School Days," "Saturday Night Fish Fry" and, from more than eleven years before, "Bounce the Ball." A jaunty bounce masks the dark lyrical undertones of "Is My Pop in There?," with a child trying to locate his father on payday—"when pop gets his pay, he always seems to go astray." Verse after verse describes the grim conditions of the household and its inhabitants—food is getting low, the landlord took the bed, baby needs some shoes. Strangely, after all of Louie's debauchery and alcohol-soaked songs, the "there" of "Is My Pop in There?" is never explicitly revealed to be a bar in the song.

Later that month, Jordan and his Tympany Five toured the Caribbean. Using the Myrtle Park Hotel in Kingston, Jamaica, as their home base, the band flew out to play Haiti, Guyana and Trinidad, in addition to the Jamaican shows. Most of the concerts were outdoors, and the crowds knew Louie's songs well. Izenhall, Tympany Five trumpeter since the mid-1940s, called the tour the highlight of all his travels with Jordan and the band. However, no one liked the food much.

Louie would continue to feature calypso numbers in his live act, recordings and films, including songs like "Fifty Cents" and a Caribbean-tinged version of "Junco Partner." And who could blame him? "Stone Cold Dead in the Market," one of Jordan's several duets with Ella Fitzgerald, was number one for five weeks. "Run Joe" was number one for two weeks. And songs like "Early in the Morning" and "Push Ka Pee She Pie (The Saga of Saga Boy)" were hits and became mainstays on his set lists through his long career.

On June 5 and 13, 1951, with Milt Gabler and an expanded band in New York City, Louie and the Tympany Five recorded the Louie-written, holiday-themed "May Every Day Be Christmas" and "Happy Birthday Boogie," though the latter was never released.

They also cut jazz journalist Leonard Feather's "How Blue Can You Get?," which B.B. King would later make into a signature hit, and several songs solidly in the Tympany Five vein—"Bone Dry," "Three Handed Woman," "Fat Sam from Birmingham," "If You're So Smart, How Come You Ain't Rich?" and "Louisville Lodge Meeting"—the latter being a "Saturday Night Fish Fry" re-write. "It was crazy" substitutes for "It was rockin'," and the setting is an "Order of the Western Star" lodge rather than a New Orleans house party. Havoc occurs when the sister membership stops by for a visit, and "ballin' and brawling" happens rather than the "scuffling and shuffling."

Augmenting the Tympany Five were trumpeters Emmett Perry and Bob Mitchell, trombonists Leon Comegys and Bob Burgess, Marty Flax on baritone sax, Oliver Nelson on alto sax, Reuben Phillips on tenor sax and Jimmy Peterson on piano. "Wild" Bill Davis got two of his songs recorded at the June 13 session, the unissued "I Love That Kind of Carryin' On" and even doing a solo vocal turn on his "Please Don't Leave Me," though Louie takes over on vocals halfway through. On July 30, Louie and the same group cut Vaughn "Choo Choo Ch'Boogie" Horton's "Cock-A-Doodle-Doo," David Saxon and Sammy Gallop's "There Must Be a Way" and Louie's own "Garmoochie," which wasn't released.

That November 28, Louie entered the studio again with a vastly beefed-up band. The ensemble included Aaron Izenhall, Emmett Perry, Bob Mitchell and Harold "Money" Johnson on trumpet; Alfred Cobbs and Bob Burgess on trombone; Oliver Nelson on alto sax; Josh Jackson and Irving "Skinny" Brown on tenor sax; Numa "Pee Wee" Moore on baritone sax; John Malachi on piano; Bill Jennings on guitar; Bob Bushnell on bass; Joe "Chris Columbus" Morris on drums; and female Tympany Five vocalist Valli Ford.

This 1951 Decca release, "Bone Dry," is notably by Louis Jordan and His Orchestra, rather than his Tympany Five. It didn't chart.

The group, billed on the Decca record as "Louis Jordan and His Orchestra," recorded a version of "All of Me" with Louie and Ford. Several tunes co-written by Louie were cut, including "Stop Making Music," the blues "Slow Down" and "Never Trust a Woman," along with the ballad "There Goes My Heart," the instrumental "Come and Get It" and the hot "Work, Baby, Work," written by Jack Adrian.

Also cut was another great novelty drinking song, "Lay Something on the Bar (Besides Your Elbow)," written by Billy Austin (of "Is You Is or Is You Ain't" and "Have You Got the Gumption" fame) and Sheldon Smith, and later issued as a single by comedian Jerry Lewis on Capitol Records. It was a productive day, with eight titles waxed and only "Stop Making Music" not released.

"Don't never trust a woman," Louie sang on his new she's-a-gold-digger song of the same name co-written with Bill Doggett, "until she's dead and deep." Despite the warning, Louie married again, on November 14, 1951, in Providence, Rhode Island, having finally divorced Fleecie Moore. The pairing of Louie and Florence "Vicky" Hayes Johnson—with whom his extramarital coupling would cost Louie thousands in legal bills, millions in royalties and very nearly his life at the hands of Fleecie—would last only through the 1950s.

As Louie's career faltered, so did he and Vicky's marriage, as he spent more time at home instead of on tour. The two separated in 1960. When he and Martha Weaver got serious, he eventually sought a divorce from Vicky.

When Louie toured with his orchestra, Valli Ford shared lead vocal duties with Louie, as well as Lloyd Smith, billed as the "Fat Man." Ford had previously sung with Duke Ellington as Sara Forde. A *Down Beat* article from September 21 notes a day in the touring life of Louie and the band:

> *The sum* [Louie] *pocketed was the staggering total of $9,000, certainly one of the highest any band has earned on a dance date anywhere, and a record for Jordan. Jordan's 14-piece band played the Sunday dance...on a $1,500 guarantee and 60 percent of the gross. Attendance was 7,005 and the admittance price $2.25. Last year, at the same spot* [the Kansas City Auditorium] *Louis made $7,700, still quite a respectable amount for a night's work. The Jordan band will be on tour until January, doing one-niters under the aegis of GAC.*

• •

Typically, the year 1952 saw changes in the Tympany Five—now composed of drummer Charlie Rice, trumpeter Bob Mitchell, pianist Jimmy Peterson, bassist Bob Bushnell and electric guitarist Bert Payne—as well as a return to the literal "Five" in the Tympany Five in the studio. Particularly, departing trumpeter Aaron Izenhall and drummer Joe "Chris Columbus" Morris had been band mainstays.

In May, in preparation of the forthcoming American presidential election, Louie recorded "Jordan for President," patterned after an old minstrel routine, "Deacon Jones for President." Over Peterson's mellow piano riff, Louie gives a political speech. He offers to entertain all U.S. kiddies on the White House lawn every Sunday at 2:30 p.m., to make sure every living American gets his portion ("after I get mine") and to get the people straight on all the candidates. He notes that Tennessean Estes Kefauver "has a good offer," and "there'll be no graft from [Robert A.] Taft." Louie thinks fellow Arkansawyer Douglas MacArthur would be great to get the military bit straight, but for Harold Stassen, he gives real praise—"a hipster who will take no sassin'"—while correctly naming Dwight Eisenhower as the "man of the hour."

However, Jordan promises an administration that will "groove you, move you, and keep you sent" on the Swing ticket, "the candidate with a beat." Before noting that incumbent President Harry S. Truman doesn't want the job, he exclaims,

"No longer will I be on a phonograph record, I'm gonna be on Congressional Record!" Best of all, on Louie's July 8 birthday, every American would get new shoes—one of Louie's favorite items. "Jordan for President" was developed into one of the Tympany Five's new concert routines. (Competing with Louis Jordan for mock candidacy for president in 1952 was Pogo the possum of newspaper comic fame and his slogan, "I Go Pogo." Gracie Allen of the Burns and Allen radio program had gotten surprising mileage out of a mock run for president in 1948 and inspired others four years later.)

Louie recorded four decidedly more mature sides with an orchestra under the direction of Nelson Riddle in February 1953: Rodgers and Hart's "I Didn't Know What Time It Was," "It's Better to Wait for Love," "Only Yesterday" and the lush, wrenching ballad "Just Like a Butterfly (That's Caught in the Rain)."

"He did ballads and very few people know it, but I loved to hear him sing ballads," Martha Jordan would later note. "He could sing a ballad."

With Louie always at the fore of musical trends, in hindsight, the formation of his big band seems a rare misstep. His own musical innovation helped put an end to the big band era—why would he attempt to revive it in the early 1950s? It's easy to suspect the orchestra was an attempt to confer more musical legitimacy upon himself, following a decade of successes mostly involving funny songs about partying and food. Louie's contemporary Louis Armstrong had recently done a similar-but-opposite 180-degree turn with his band. Armstrong pared down his band in the late 1940s to more closely resemble his Hot Five and Seven ensembles of the 1920s, to renewed artistic vigor and acclaim.

Down Beat writer Leonard Feather reviewed the Jordan big band's performance at the Rustic Cabin in Englewood Cliffs, New Jersey:

> *Always a perfect showman, Louis is in complete command of this enlarged crew. Surprisingly, he did some of his best singing of the evening on ballads. Such tunes as "Trust In Me," "Morning Side of the Mountain" and "Don't Let the Sun Catch You Crying" seemed to indicate that this neglected aspect of his personality could seriously cut into the King Cole market…If* [the big band] *stays together during 1952, as seems likely, it could easily develop into one of the country's top 10.*

The musical switch "with the type of backing usually accorded Nat Cole or Perry Como" caused commotion among his fans, if a *Down Beat* article from June 1953 is to be believed. "Will you please tell people," Louie asked the reporter, "that I'm not changing my style, not going to go on the road with a full orchestra and strings, and that I'm not looking to do a single [act]. That record was just an experiment."

Louie asserted that a couple weeks after his big band's debut, he started getting letters asking if he were becoming a pop singer now. "A lot of people were thinking I was going to quit working with my band," he claimed. "But that isn't the way it is. I'm happy the way I've been working."

In truth, Louie's big band "experiment" was expensive to maintain and—unsurprising, since the era's peak had passed—not wildly popular, especially compared to the Tympany Five. Despite Louie's quotes protesting his seriousness behind the big band, it was something he had long wanted to do.

Louie's big band dream was something Louie's manager Berle Adams had always been against, "our one big battle," Adams said. Had it been successful, one can imagine Louie happily continuing on with the full orchestra—and welcoming the sense of greater musical legitimacy bestowed upon him as much as the broader musical range.

No doubt adding to the confusion was that Louie did temporarily dissolve the Tympany Five at the beginning of 1952 on doctor's advice due to Louie's arthritis. Louie relaxed at his Phoenix, Arizona home but not for long. A July 1952 article in *Down Beat* described Louie's current stage show:

> *Louis sang "Work, Baby, Work," and Louis swung "Wheel of Fortune" and Louis' two beautiful girls* [Elaine Robinson and Ann Bailey], *who are so lovely to look at that nobody notices whether they can sing, did a jump blues. And Louis did his wonderful version of "Junco Partner," and finally his eight Jordanettes danced and everybody came onstage for the calypso finale, "You Will Always Have A Friend." And through it all Louis didn't sing or play a single note of bad music.*

Louie toured through the end of 1952 and played a residency at the Golden Hotel in Reno, Nevada, with his success there helping do away with a color line that found few black bands performing in Reno, Lake Tahoe or Las Vegas at the time. Louie and the entourage then played the San Francisco Paramount and flopped into Los Angeles for a much-needed rest.

Looming after the break was the "Biggest Show of 1953," a coast-to-coast tour lasting well over a month. This massive undertaking featured four headliners—Frankie Laine, Ella Fitzgerald, Woody Herman and His Orchestra (also known for "Caldonia Boogie," though less successfully than Louie) and Louis Jordan and his Tympany Five. Additionally appearing on the bill were Frank Marlowe, Bobby Ephram and Dusty Fletcher (also known

This 1953 advertisement touts the long relationship between Louis Jordan, his booking agency and his record company. But that perfect orbit would soon spin out of control. *Courtesy Old State House Museum.*

for "Open the Door, Richard," though less successfully than Louie). Among the dozens of dates across the country on the tour was a long string of one-nighters through the American Midwest and East in addition to several West Coast dates up into Canada. No big thing for seasoned road warriors like the Tympany Five, but everyone was looking forward to a few days' break before the "Biggest Show" tour. That included Tympany Five pianist and chief arranger Jimmy Peterson. He'd recorded such tunes as the calypso "Time Marches On," "Junco Partner," "Oil Well, Texas," "Azure-Te" and "Jordan for President" with Louie and the band the previous year. Peterson and a new member of the band's entourage who had been a security guard set out in the Tympany Five vehicle to visit friends.

Outside Reno, the vehicle rolled off the road into water, turning completely over. The vehicle was totaled. The band's arrangements were ruined. Peterson, the Tympany Five pianist/arranger, was killed.

Louie had already been planning on making some changes in the Tympany Five—his long-standing insistence on pre-show sobriety, the highest musicianship and showmanship and, of course, lengthy rehearsals always made for a volatile mix with his musicians—but not like this. He commissioned a new book of arrangements to be written and hired Lexington, Mississippi native Chester Lane to play piano. Louie and Lane had known each other since their oil boom days playing in Bob Alexander's Harmony Kings. (Chester Lane's son, Chester Lane Jr., would eventually coach at Arkansas Baptist College, founded in 1884 and located on High Street in Little Rock, which Louie always claimed to have attended. Louie was such a generous donor to the college, especially to the school's choir, who would quibble?)

Louie took the opportunity to change the rhythm section, too. Johnny Kirkwood, in his mid-twenties, became the youngest member of the band, replacing Charlie Rice on drums, and Thurber "Sam Guy" Jay replaced Bob Bushnell on bass. Rice had been around about as long as Peterson—a year or so. Bushnell had been in the band for around three years and played on many Decca Tympany Five sessions, including "Blue Light Boogie," the Louis Armstrong duets and an Ella Fitzgerald duet session. Bassist Thurber Jay would soon be required to play the newfangled electric bass instead of the stand-up bass if he wanted to keep his job in the Tympany Five. Jay compensated for the sudden change by tilting the instrument's neck up slightly, closer to where a stand-up's neck might be, and thus was able to stay on in the band—for a while.

Chapter 9

"I'M AT THE TOP OF THE HILL, AND ON THE WAY DOWN"

Louie's perfect orbit, which had revolved so successfully for so long, was now spinning out of control.

Berle Adams—Louie's manager, promoter, fan, mainstay and, perhaps most importantly, a key arbiter of Tympany Five song material—was leaving the fold. He had been there when Louie was nobody—and when Adams himself was nobody as well. He had encouraged the novelty material that had, for better or worse, defined the image of Louis Jordan and his Tympany Five. Louie and Adams had risen together to create the Tympany Five aesthetic, to sell millions of records, to make movies, to sell out concerts across the country, to rise to the top of show business, to create a new genre—and to profoundly impact American culture.

But Adams had received an offer he couldn't refuse from MCA—although he admits the salary "was a fraction of what I earned with Jordan and my publishing and record business"—and he was having health issues and desired the security such a corporate position could offer. Adams would become a powerhouse at MCA, launching its international TV division in the late 1950s, signing such artists to MCA as the Who, Elton John and Olivia Newton-John in the 1960s and 1970s and even helping an MCA colleague negotiate the acquisition of American football team the New York Titans, subsequently renamed the Jets. Adams died in 2009 at ninety-two.

Just prior to accepting the job, Adams had dinner with Louie "to explain the MCA offer and my decision. He said, 'Well, Berle, I guess you feel that

This GAC advertisement highlights Louis Jordan's success as a writer, performer, recording artist and—with hundreds of teens queuing around the block to see him—the "King of the Bobby Sock Brigade."

I'm at the top of the hill, and on the way down.' [Adams] asked how he could say that…It was a rough meeting."

Still, the two remained friendly, and some months later, Louie invited Adams to see him perform with the full orchestra when they were headlining at the Brooklyn Theater in Brooklyn. "He invited me to come and listen. After the show, I joined Louie for dinner," Adams said. "He never asked my opinion of the band; he knew the answer."

However, Louie was incredibly prescient about the state of his career, at least as far as Decca Records was concerned. After more than fifteen years, not counting his time with the label as a player with Chick Webb, his contract was not renewed. His final Decca session, on January 4, 1954, included another telling item—the Chester Lane–arranged recording of "Nobody Knows You When You're Down and Out." It was a 1920s-era blues Louie would have recalled from his youth—and apparently thought appropriate.

• • • • • • • • • • • • • • • • • • • •

Louie's post-Decca time must have often seemed surprisingly tough to him. After his unprecedented success through most of the previous decade, the question often arises why Louie wasn't able to continue with his popularity or even expand it as musical styles opened up through the 1950s—regardless of for which label he was recording. In retrospect, it seems it must have been more than Jordan's exploded triumvirate of Decca Records, Milt Gabler and Berle Adams. Louie had long been influential but was now pushed out of the marketplace by those he had influenced. It wasn't so different as when Louie had stormed the charts himself the previous decade and others had to make room.

Could "Louis Jordan" have been so successfully associated as the "Global Favorite of eleven million GIs" that the name would need to be relegated to the same memory hole where rationing, victory gardens, recycling, passenger trains and moves toward racial and gender equality were buried in postwar America? Divides between urban and rural—barnyard songs and city hipster songs being other rich Tympany Five topics—were also being blurred as the concept of suburbs emerged.

Meanwhile, artists such as Amos Milburn, Wynonie Harris, Joe Liggins and his Honeydrippers and others took the drunken hipster persona that Louis Jordan and his Tympany Five had patented on vinyl and made it their own.

However, the new rock and R&B sounds captivating the country, which Louie developed and refined during his Decca years, would scarcely be found on the American major labels like Decca during the late 1940s and early 1950s. More nimble independent labels, with much lower sales figures needed to keep them in the black, began to rise—Chess and Vee-Jay in Chicago, Illinois; King in Cincinnati, Ohio; Sun in Memphis, Tennessee; Specialty and Modern in Los Angeles, California; Atlantic in New York City, New York; and Duke/Peacock in Houston, Texas.

(An undated letter written by Louie to Duke/Peacock owner Don Robey on stationery from New York's Hotel Sharon shows Louie ready to sign with Robey's Peacock record label, which launched in Houston in 1949: "Like we discussed, it is my intention to come with you on Peacock when my contract is up with Decca and in the event this materializes, I hope it will give Peacock a boost and I think there's a chance for us both to make some money." After further discussing a curious payment of $10,000 by Louis to Robey, Louis is generous: "About paying me on the next tour we will cross that bridge when we get to it, as you might find the first year a bit rough. I'm not exactly hurting right now." It's unknown why the deal with Robey didn't occur.)

Even more directly, Decca Records signee Bill Haley and the Comets had teamed up with Louie's Decca producer, Milt Gabler, to hit the rock 'n' roll zeitgeist, including recording a cover of "Choo Choo Ch'Boogie." "I asked the whole group [the Comets] to project the way that Jordan's group had done," Gabler said in 1991.

Louie's former manager was less circumspect: "That record ["Rock Around the Clock"] was an out-and-out steal," Berle Adams said. "Milt Gabler admitted that he told Haley to listen to Jordan records and imitate Jordan's shuffle beat."

With Louie's dismissal from Decca, the label banking on the combination of Tympany Five producer Gabler, the Tympany Five shuffle and Bill Haley for rock 'n' roll music seems like short-sighted opportunism at best. Too bad Louie's vocal and musical authority couldn't have been utilized to claim some ownership of the new sounds—for Louie as well as Decca.

But Louie had other recording options. He'd signed to Aladdin Records and indeed had already begun recording for the company in November 1953, a couple months before his final Decca sessions.

Louie's Aladdin output covers familiar territory—songs about drinking, food and out-of-control women, with a few ballads and a couple instrumentals thrown in for balance. Louie gives it his usual go, but the material as a whole pales even to his lesser Decca songs. Among the exceptions are the typical partying rockers "I'll Die Happy" and "Whiskey Do Your Stuff"; the ballads "'Til We Two Are One," "It's Hard to Be

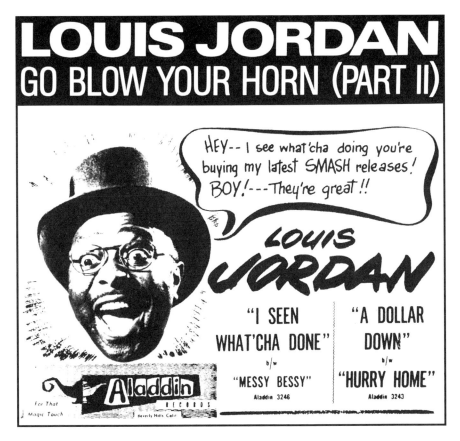

Aladdin, to which Louis Jordan signed after leaving Decca, experimented with ten-inch albums in 1954. By the early 1960s, Aladdin had folded. This ten-inch French reissue was released in 1983. *Courtesy Stephanie Smittle.*

Good Without You" and "Hurry Home"; as well as the hard-driving blues "If I Had Any Sense, I'd Go Back Home."

On the latter, Louie's vocal nearly aches, giving believability to lyrics from a man who realizes "fortune and fame is not for me, and all these pretty stories ain't what they cooked up to be" but who "didn't have the will power to stop" and had to do what he had to do.

If Louie found any autobiography in the words, his time in the desert far from the hit parade was just beginning. He did a half dozen sessions for Aladdin but couldn't find a hit.

Chapter 10

"DOC, IT'S ROCK 'N' ROLL"

L ouis Jordan was apprehensive of new material," says Berle Adams. "Perhaps it was coincidental that after I left him, his flow of hit records diminished. No fresh material, no record sales. Louis Jordan preferred me to book the dates and screen the new songs."

By March 1955, Louie was already recording for RCA-Victor Records, a major label that would soon be home to the emerging king of rock 'n' roll, Elvis Presley. By the end of the same year, Bill Haley had sold some three million records for Decca. Louie's releases were issued on (relegated to?) the short-lived RCA subsidiary labels Vik and "X." Again, food, partying and women remain the dominant subject matter, but here the songwriting seems a notch higher. And as usual, Louie's underrated balladry—"Where Can I Go," "Whatever Lola Wants"—remains exceptional. "Bananas" hits on two of Louie's themes: food and a calypso flavor.

Recorded in Hollywood on October 18, 1955, the song "Rock 'n' Roll Call," with its refrain "reading and writing is good enough, rock 'n' roll beats all that stuff," gives the impression that Louie is hip to the new beat. Only this, the second of the three RCA sessions, featured a Tympany Five–style band setup with Chester Lane on piano, John Kirkwood on drums, Thurber Jay on bass, Bert Payne on guitar, Bob Mitchell on trumpet and Lowell Hastings on second saxophone. "Baby You're Just Too Much," "Chicken Back" and "Where Can I Go," written by Louie and Clyde Jones, came from this session. In "Where Can I Go," a slow blues, Louie convincingly sings the tale of a man searching for peace of mind.

The first and third sessions, both held in New York City, were augmented with additional musicians: Frank Grillo, Francisco Pozo, Rafael Miranda, Maurice Simon, Jerome Richardson and David McRae on March 18, 1956, and Hindai Butts, Heywood Henry, Reuben Phillips, Seldon Powell, Lewis Albert Martin, Olivette Miller and vocalist/conga player Dottie Smith on April 17, 1956. The first session produced "Let's Do It Up Baby" and "Slow, Smooth and Easy"—both written by Winfield Scott, future author of "Return to Sender"—as well as Nellie Lutcher's "It's Been Said," "Lola" and "Bananas." The latter attempt produced three songs, "Hard Head," "Texas Stew" and "A Man Ain't a Man," all penned by Eddie "Tex" Curtis, who conducted the session.

Bizarrely, Louie's final session for the label in April 1956 even featured a harp player (Olivette Miller) plucking along with the blues. Louis had recorded a dozen sides for RCA and, again, had little chart action to show for it. His efforts for both ill-fated RCA subsidiaries Vik and "X" stiffed. He and the label parted ways.

That same month, over on RCA Records proper, Presley's "Heartbreak Hotel" sold one million copies.

Rock 'n' roll was on, and now the major labels had a piece. Capitalism was co-opting the rebellion.

· · · · · · · · · · · · · · · · · · · ·

Meanwhile, Chuck Berry was studying Louie's guitarist, fellow St. Louis, Missourian Carl Hogan, who Berry described as an "idol." Describing the "Chuck Berry riff," Berry's signature guitar figure heard at the opening of "Johnny B. Goode" and others of his classics, Berry said, "The first time I heard that was in one of Carl Hogan's riffs in Louis Jordan's band."

Berry expounded on how Hogan influenced his own guitar playing in an unused 1987 interview for the Berry biopic *Hail! Hail! Rock 'n' Roll*: "Louis Jordan's guitarist, Carl Hogan, was the inspiration for most of my solos—'Carol,' 'Johnny B. Goode,' 'Roll Over, Beethoven,'" Chuck Berry told guitarist Robbie Robertson and then hummed the well-known "Chuck Berry riff."

"He had something like this in the center of a solo," Berry explained, "and I opened my song[s] with it. 'Roll Over Beethoven,' after it hit, later on, 'Johnny B. Goode' hit, 'Carol' hit, with the same solo. A little difference in the figure, but the same principles."

In 2013, Robertson said, "I've had the opportunity to sit with Chuck Berry and say, 'OK, on Tuesday, it was Teresa Brewer and Patti Page singing popular music. On Thursday, something happened and there you were, and Little Richard and Fats Domino. Were you guys just waiting in the wings? How did rock 'n' roll explode that quickly? What happened?' And Chuck Berry said because the real father of rock 'n' roll had taught us something we couldn't wait to share with everybody, and that guy's name was Louis Jordan."

Martha said she doesn't think Chuck Berry and Louie ever met, although, coincidentally, she and Berry knew each other in high school back in St. Louis but weren't in the same cliques, or as she says, they were not "boon coons."

In his 1987 autobiography, Berry describes a revelation he'd had by the late 1940s that also would have been familiar to Louie: "I realized I had to have something to attract a club owner over the musicians they were used to. I decided to add little gimmicks I had observed here and there to my songs to try and sell my bit. One was making gestures that complemented the lyrics, such as squatting low to do a passage in a song that was sentimental and bluesy; another was to deliver facial expressions that pronounced the nature of the lyrics. I could tell from the response that it was going over."

Other new artists on the scene, such as Bo Diddley, also acknowledged Louie's influence: "Louis Jordan was the cat I tried to be most like."

Louie played a series of dates with another rising star who grew up worshiping the music of the Tympany Five, this time an up-and-comer in the blues field, guitarist B.B. King. "Louis was remarkable," King told author John Chilton in 1991, "because I think he was so far ahead of his time—what he was doing became the origins of rap. He was rhyming things that nobody else was able to do," said King. "I idolized his talent."

King had first gotten turned on to Louie's music hearing it on KWEM radio in West Memphis, Arkansas. The first time he got to see Louie live, B.B. and his teenaged date and future wife, Martha—whom he asked to marry him that night—were too young to get in the club. They had to peep through the slats of the Jones Night Spot, which was an eight-mile walk from the Indianola, Mississippi plantation where King worked.

King described the scene: "Seeing him through the peepholes was incredible: His bug eyes, his golden alto sax, his strut onstage…Me and Martha we were laughing up a storm, tapping our feet, having a great time looking at all the dancing couples dressed to the teeth, smooching and swinging to the music, when I felt good enough to turn to my girl and kiss her."

When King got his first on-air radio gig, pitching Pepticon tonic on Memphis, Tennessee's WDIA, the first songs he performed were his old reliables—Louie's "Somebody Done Changed the Lock on My Door" and "Buzz Me." From the 1960s through the 1980s, King regularly covered both Tympany Five hits and obscurities on his albums, from "Buzz Me," "Caldonia," "We Can't Agree" and "Let the Good Times Roll" on down to "Inflation Blues," "I Know What You're Puttin' Down," "Teardrops from My Eyes" and "Heed My Warning." In addition to adopting Louie's "Let the Good Times Roll" as his own signature opening concert song, King had particular success with "How Blue Can You Get?" with its lyrical punch line, "I gave you seven children, now you want to give them back!"

"I think it was Louis Jordan who made the real marriage between jump-band blues and barrelhouse blues," King wrote in his 1994 autobiography. "Every musician I knew—singer or saxist, guitarist or drummer—idolized Louis Jordan. First, he was funny. Whether he was talking 'bout 'Nobody Here But Us Chickens' or 'Reet, Petite and Gone,' Louis made you laugh. And, then, he made you dance. He had witty lyrics and irresistible rhythm. Plus, he was novel. He proved you can take the blues in a dozen different directions and keep 'em blue."

King had long recorded for MCA Records, which, conveniently, already owned the rights to Louie's Decca recordings and stood to gain the most from any boost in the Tympany Five back catalogue caused by a King tribute record.

In 1999, King released his long-promised Louis Jordan tribute album, *Let the Good Times Roll: The Music of Louis Jordan*, with a full eighteen Jordan songs, only a few of which King had recorded before. King's label, MCA Records, also commissioned a documentary film on the recording of the tribute album. Lol Creme, formerly of the English pop-rock band 10cc, shot and edited an hour-long piece in black and white. Despite high praise of the film from many of the participants, the documentary was never aired.

In the jazz world, Sonny Rollins had become one of the most influential modern jazz saxophonists. "But," Rollins admitted, "I really loved Louis Jordan and his band, the Tympany Five. That is the first time I was exposed to the saxophone."

Rollins described first seeing Louie: "I loved the way Louis Jordan's saxophone looked. But I liked his music first. Then I saw a picture of him in a club across the street from my elementary school; he was posing with a King Zephyr alto saxophone. It is such a beautiful instrument!" Rollins got an alto sax from his doting mother on account of his fascination with Louie. He later described Louie as "a bridge between the blues and jazz."

Much like the arm's length he gave rock 'n' roll, Louie could not get behind the dissonant bebop that Rollins helped create—and certainly not the anti-showmanship moves such as turning of one's back on audiences embraced by Miles Davis and the genre's other practitioners.

Rollins explained the thought process behind the beboppers: "My friends and I believed that bebop was the first musical movement to completely turn away from the minstrel image of most black entertainment. It was a complete opposite, and it was a new birth of freedom. It was more than music—it was a social movement, and we wanted to be part of it. We didn't want to be 'entertainers,' per se; we wanted to be serious musicians."

One can imagine what Louie, once literally a minstrel, who existed only to entertain his audiences, thought of such talk.

• • • • • • • • • • • • • • • • • • • •

In other music circles, the music of Louis Jordan was also being acknowledged. Guitarist Freddie King (no relation to B.B.) explained that he learned to play his instrument trying to imitate Tympany Five horn lines. Freddie King, along with Chuck Berry, would be among the main American electric guitarists influencing the coming wave of English blues-rockers like John Mayall, Eric Clapton, Keith Richards, Jeff Beck, Peter Green, John Lennon, Paul McCartney and many others.

And James Brown, who would emerge as R&B's most important voice, simply said this about Louie: "He was everything!"

Brown gives a quote similar to Chuck Berry's in terms of their learned showmanship: "I learned early on that the key to making it in show business, especially in the form of a revue, was all in the presentation of whatever material you had."

Brown once outlined the three elements found in the roots of a James Brown performance: 1. "The immortal Louis Jordan," 2. comic books, and 3. Gorgeous George. In fact, James Brown would emerge as the most vocal—and most successful—of Jordan's immediate followers cum successors: "I still think that the best showman of them all was Louis Jordan," Brown said in one of his autobiographies, in a passage describing where he got his ideas on performing. "Louis Jordan was *the* man in those days, though a lot of people have forgotten it. His stuff was popular with blacks *and* whites," Brown says.

"What killed me was when I found out he was not only the sax player, but the writer, producer, and arranger as well," Brown said, perhaps overestimating Louie's control of Decca studios, if not Louie's capabilities.

"His songs were filled with stories and fanciful tales, mostly about women, and shrieks and stomps and abrupt rhythmic changes and tightly choreographed jumps and moves. His stuff was, in many ways, the true precursor to what young black performers today call rap music...I took a lot from Louis Jordan, and hoped to model myself in his image, because in my mind, he was the best," Soul Brother #1 remarked about his idol, Mr. Jordan.

"His talent was so awesome," Brown said. "I thought it had to be supernatural."

Michael Jackson—whose father was also an Arkansas native and whom one could argue had taken over the mantle of the most popular crossover musician that Brown had taken over from Louie—said at Brown's December 2006 funeral, "James Brown is my greatest inspiration." So here we have a direct line from the Father of R&B to the Godfather of Soul to the King of Pop.

Despite his major hand in its creation, Louie professed to abhor the new beats and the musical low bar—much like Dr. Frankenstein hated and feared his monster.

"We emphasized the beat," Louie told Leonard Feather in *Down Beat* magazine in 1969, "mostly through a shuffle boogie rhythm. The only thing that really changed was the intensity of the beat, particularly in the drums. Later they brought the bass up, and then the guitar, which more or less came into its own with the rock 'n' rollers."

Others from the old guard with far less culpability in rock 'n' roll's development, such as Frank Sinatra, took criticism of the musical style even further, calling it made for, and by, "cretins" and insinuating it caused juvenile delinquency.

This musical judgment was light compared to the right-wingers, race-baiters and other cultural warriors in that emerging American field of industry who claimed to find R&B and rock abhorrent on not just musical but also societal levels. Claims from these groups that this music was providing the youthful soundtrack to questioning the too-slowly fading Jim Crow tradition fueled literal fires of offending records through the 1970s and 1980s—before their sights turned to rap music.

Knowing what we know about Louie, it's safe to assume that his concerns about eroding musicianship were legitimate, but he and other naysayers were surely just as concerned about losing their cultural primacy.

In Louie's case, again, these concerns were prescient. "The music didn't change as much as the rhythm," Louie asserted. "More noise, more amplification—they just put more juice behind everything. On some of the records in the early stages of rock 'n' roll, you could hardly hear the melody, nor the singer. Noise can hide a gang of faults. That's just about the reason why amplification got bigger—because so many people made records who couldn't even sing."

Journalist Feather admits that Louie never had any musical faults to cover but is quick to add that Jordan's analysis may be debatable. Even from the vantage point of the late 1960s, Feather kindly doesn't note that Louie's own recordings "in the early stages of rock 'n' roll" for Mercury in the late 1950s were similarly noisy, with intense beats, loud bass and guitar and the vocal often buried in the mix—although the sessions were with the most famous producer Louie would ever work with, Quincy Jones, and with a raft of well-regarded session men mostly redoing the Tympany Five's best-known songs.

Ironically, the label was started by Louie's old manager, Berle Adams. And, as Adams explains, the irony of Louie recording for Mercury compounds: "When I founded Mercury Records, Louis Jordan declared that he would like to switch labels and join me. I was tongue-tied by the gracious and sincere offer. Here was one of the biggest-selling record artists volunteering to reduce his royalty income by moving to a new label in order to help his friend," Adams says.

"Selfishly, as an investor and an executive, I should have been receptive to his offer, knowing that his name would jump-start our new company," he notes. However, long-established major label Decca Records had superior distribution, which meant more money for Louie. Adams wasn't being totally selfless—more money and more royalties also, of course, meant more money for Louie's manager: Adams himself. But Adams also felt he "would still be hanging on to [Louie's] coattails" should Louie join Mercury at that time: "His success would be good for the company, but not for me."

Adams thus found himself in a nice negotiating position. The possibility that Louie could join his then-manager's new label left Decca executives eager to play ball to retain their star. "When I sat down with [Decca's] Jack and David Kapp and outlined the new Jordan deal," Adams says, "it was approved without hesitation, and Jordan lived richly for many years thereafter. I was lucky to be working with someone who had the character and trust of Louis Jordan."

When Louie actually later did sign with Mercury, Adams had since divested from the company, and he hadn't managed Louie for more than five years.

Louie's first Mercury sessions were in October 1956 in New York City. He'd also signed with a new personal manager, Ben C. Waller. The Tympany Five included Mickey Baker (of Mickey and Sylvia; the duo would record "Love Is Strange" the same month) on the ever-important and, here, loudly mixed electric guitar. Also included were Tennessee natives Sam "The Man" Taylor on tenor sax and Jimmy Cleveland on trombone, Ernie Royal on trumpet, Ernie Hayes on piano, Charlie Persip on drums, Wendell Marshall on bass and Albert "Budd" Johnson on tenor and baritone sax.

The main order of the day was to collect more modern arrangements of Tympany Five classics onto the new format—the 33⅓-rpm long-playing record album—using improved recording techniques and equipment.

At this point, Louie's classic multimillion sellers like "Choo Choo Ch'Boogie" and "Is You Is or Is You Ain't" had been not only off the hit parade but also generally unavailable for purchase for a decade. But two new songs were also cut for a promotional (that is, not available on the LP) single for the album—"Big Bess" backed with "Cat Scratchin'." Although "Big Bess" opens promisingly enough by aping the opening riffs of "Beans and Cornbread," both "Bess" and "Cat Scratchin'" are fairly average takes along the well-known lyrical topics of women and partying, respectively. Furthermore—incredibly—initial Mercury Records promo materials for the single misspelled Louie's last name as "Jordon."

Louie manages to pull off a new twist or two in reconstructing his old hits—"Don't Let the Sun Catch You Crying" particularly benefits from a fresh arrangement and added guitar. But as a whole, the reworkings are decidedly inferior. "Beware," with its intricate, clever rhyme scheme, is taken so fast it is rendered unintelligible. The tale of "Run Joe" is taken at such a clip that it, too, gets buried in the mix. The emphasis away from the patented Tympany Five shuffle essentially removes the essence of what made it interesting and different in the first place.

Louie's first Mercury album was called *Somebody Up There Digs Me*. The label began billing Louie as the "Original Rock and Roller." "Man, I'm Swingin' Again!" Louie exclaims in one Mercury advertisement promoting the "Big Bess" single.

When fans proved uninterested in musical history lessons, the sessions for Louie's next Mercury album, *Man, We're Wailin'*, relied less on songs he'd successfully waxed previously. But rather than engaging new material, the tilt was toward pop fare and standards such as "Sweet Lorraine," popularized by Nat "King" Cole; "Route 66"; "I Never Had a Chance"; "The Nearness of You"; and "I Hadn't Anyone Til You." With placid song choices such as these, it might seem that Mercury was hedging its bets. It could have the "Original Rock and Roller," with all his classic hits, as well as an artist with a mature sound as typified by the likes of Cole and Sinatra, who were also navigating the cultural shifts—an entire new "youth" market had emerged along with rock 'n' roll music. The grim war years of the previous decade were quickly, willfully, becoming ancient American history.

Also included was a tame mid-tempo take on "Got My Mojo Working," with cascading Jackie Davis organ and distracting backing vocals, at around the time bluesman Muddy Waters was popularizing a hot, uptempo live version, and Eddie "Tex" Curtis's "A Man Ain't a Man," which Louie had recorded just a year before for RCA. These songs leaned heavily on the organ sounds of Jackie Davis, who had replaced pianist Chester Lane. Louie thought adding electric organ would give the band a fresh sound and suggested it to Lane; Lane wanted to stick to piano. Hence, Lane exited the Tympany Five.

Dottie Smith was given a solo vocal turn on the song "Route 66" and a feature bit in "A Man Ain't a Man." A good conga player and very attractive, Smith was a welcome onstage diversion. "Route 66" was a concert staple for the band. Another pair of Jordan-credited mid-tempo instrumentals, "The Slop" and "The Jamf," were also recorded for Mercury, showcasing the band, which was rounded out by Martin Oliver on drums, Billy Hadnott on bass and Irving Ashby on guitar.

("Jamf" is an old slang acronym for "Jive Ass Motherfuckers." Even staid Louis Jordan had his bawdy moments, though the song is not nearly as wild as its title might suggest.)

One truly bright spot was an all-too-rare new song, "Rock Doc," recorded in New York City on January 25, 1957—at the single session held devoted solely to new material. Three songs came of this session: "Fire," "Ella Mae" and "Rock Doc." "Ella Mae" treads on the all-too-familiar lyrical territory of a woman out of control. "Fire" ("I'm scorchin' over you!") begins and ends with an annoying fire truck siren; the song embodies all that is wrong with Louie's Mercury material: too loud, too fast and trying too hard.

But Louie soars on "Rock Doc." Mercury released it as a single in which the protagonist extols the greatness of rock 'n' roll to his incredulous psychoanalyst, who repeatedly attempts to do word-association tests with his ever-rocking patient. If Louie was holding his nose while singing another paean to rock 'n' roll with "Rock Doc," one would never know. "Rock, doc! Rock 'n' roll!," he sings. "A man's gotta wail or lose control! Rock 'em, roll 'em—doc, it's rock 'n' roll!"

Around the time, Louie made television appearances on the variety shows of Ed Sullivan, Jackie Gleason, Milton Berle, Perry Como and Steve Allen, among others. The latter appearance in August 1956 on Allen's program came while Louie and the band were playing the Mocambo in San Francisco, California. It was an early coast-to-coast live TV hookup—Allen, in New York, introduced Louie and the band, in San Francisco, to the general

This "greatest hits" album was issued by Decca in 1958, well after Louis Jordan had left the label. "The whole time I was at Decca," Jordan said, "they were so busy making money with my singles that they never thought about albums, so I missed out on that."

bemusement regarding the cross-continental technological novelty of host, studio audience and presumably those watching at home. Surrounded by onlookers on the street, the band is dressed in matching (of course) dark striped suits, with Louie sporting a fedora. They perform on a city streetcar turntable and race through a blisteringly fast "Caldonia Boogie," perhaps to compensate for the song being more than a decade old. As buxom Dottie Smith bangs on the congas and Louie does high kicks while blowing the saxophone, a couple of rogue jitterbuggers try to get in on the act by dancing in front of the band. While still playing the sax, Louie shoos off one dancer, only to have another fill the space. At that point, Louie motions to the policeman in the crowd for assistance. The perfectionist Louie never missed a beat, but he wasn't pleased with the visual disruption. After the whirl through "Caldonia," they play a departing cadence and exit on a streetcar, which had impeded on the Tympany Five's performance space in a more scripted fashion than the dancers, all while encouraging everyone to join them on the car as it chugs away.

However, despite such exposure—and though he and the band continued to do well on the concert circuit—once again, record-buyers remained unimpressed with Louie's mid-1950s musical stylings. In his autobiography, Quincy Jones laments his inability to score a hit for his childhood hero, Louis Jordan—or for anyone at that point—in his burgeoning career as a record producer. Still, Decca got the message and collected and reissued Louie's original 78 rpm hits on a long-playing record. It was the first of myriad re-packagings that Decca and its subsequent corporate owners would do with Louie's music over the decades. With Decca having long since paid for the recordings, the reissues were nearly guaranteed to make a profit—and they did. Louie received earnings from such—as did Fleecie Moore for that matter—and that was fine, but Louie needed a *new* hit.

Chapter 11

"SO WHO'S THE FOOL?"

Berle Adams, Louie's former manager, makes an assertion against the conventional wisdom but one that cuts close to many of Louie's post-Decca recordings:

> *Many speculate that* [Louie's chart] *decline resulted both from changes in the music business and Louie's inability to adapt to changes in musical tastes.*
>
> *I disagree. Jordan was not only a musician, he was also a great entertainer. With the right material, he would have remained at the top of his profession. It would have been easy for Louie to change his instrumentation and his rhythm, and his great sense of showmanship would have kept him in the spotlight. I believe that the secret to Jordan's success was his interpretation of outstanding comedy material. The lack of new material did him in, and for a long time I felt bad about his decline and guilty of deserting my good friend. I had been the conduit to new material throughout his climb to the top and helped to keep him there.*

If Louie sensed any cracks in the foundation, he was still highly regarded in his hometown of Brinkley, which proclaimed September 10, 1957, to be Louis Jordan Day, with Louie and the Tympany Five to play a pair of homecoming concerts. The National Guard armory show was for whites, and the Marion Anderson school gym show was for blacks.

The *Brinkley Citizen* newspaper said the event "promises to be one of the most auspicious occasions in the city's history" and described the band of "native son" and "world-famous bandleader" thus: "The celebrated Tympany Five, featuring Capitol recording star Jackie Davis at the Hammond organ, Dottie Smith on vocals and Austin Powell, noted guitarist and baritone singer." Davis had been asked to join the band specifically because of his modern-sounding organ; Powell had previously been in the band the Cats and the Fiddle.

Louie paid a visit to Arkansas Baptist College in Little Rock, where he was hailed as an alum and benefactor who had reached the top—despite all evidence against him being much of a student there. In Brinkley, he was fêted and visited with old friends as well as his father, James.

Taking up newspaper space elsewhere in Arkansas and the country was the burgeoning student racial integration situation at Central High School in Little Rock. School integration had peacefully occurred elsewhere in America and Arkansas in wake of the U.S. Supreme Court's *Brown v. Board of Education* decision, but events converged that made Central a high-profile test case, and noisy right-wingers descended on the state's capital city with signs equating race-mixing to Communism and other such ill-informed notions. The ugly scene in Little Rock made international headlines as well as the front page of the *New York Times* most of that month and was used as Cold War Communist propaganda to demonstrate American hypocrisy toward its own stated ideals. The *Arkansas Gazette* newspaper of Little Rock wryly noted in an editorial that some protestors had to ask directions to Central High—demonstrating their previous lack of interest in educational matters.

The state of Arkansas had had an occasionally moderate record on race relations, but Governor Orval Faubus had been challenging the authority of President Dwight Eisenhower to enforce racial integration. Faubus, Arkansas' thirty-sixth governor, had a liberal background, even attending the socialist Commonwealth College in Polk County, Arkansas, for three months when he was a youth. His father, Sam Faubus, had been a socialist in rural Madison County, Arkansas, and—some might be astonished to learn—long taught racial equality at home.

Arkansas governor from 1955 to 1967, Faubus held the office longer than any other in the state and ran for the office several times afterward. It has been often considered that Faubus acted in the interest of political expediency rather than his true convictions in the Central High imbroglio, but the end result was the same.

Faubus spent much of his public time following his failed showdown against the federal government attempting to atone for the situation he had created, which continues to mar the global reputation of Little Rock and the state.

Things between Faubus and Eisenhower had been coming to a head when Louie came to his Brinkley hometown to be honored. The tensions understandably cast a pall on his home state visit, although—in typical fashion—Louie never issued a public statement on the situation. In reflection and understatement, Louie later simply said of American Jim Crow racism as a whole, "I didn't agree with what was happening, but I had to take it."

In 1973, he described playing for segregated U.S. audiences in his Tympany Five heyday: "I made just as much money off white people as I did off colored. I could play a white joint this week and a colored next," he said.

"Any time I played a white theater, my black following was there. [It could be] a colored theater, but white people came to see me…Many nights, we had more white than colored, because my records were geared to the white as well as colored, and they came to hear me do my records."

By the 1950s, the rumblings that some of the showmanship elements derived from vaudeville and minstrelsy by Louie and others of his generation were "Tomming" had become conventional wisdom. The younger generations were wondering if, indeed, they "had to take it." Stars had begun using their bully pulpits to seek better treatment in the press and elsewhere; others were pressured to do so. It was not a role that Louie was comfortable in, even as it became more accepted in the 1960s and could have even placed him back on the cultural landscape.

By the early 1970s, Louie said in an interview, "Let me say this—there's many incidents down South where if the people had talked different, there wouldn't have been an incident." While not actually mentioning it, he seems defensive of any perceived low profile he might have on the race issue, noting "one thing I learned at home"—his grandmother's sticks-and-stones philosophy.

"They knew they didn't have to fight me," Louie said. "I made a whole lot of money and the white people helped me to make *more* money. So who's the fool?"

Contrasting Louie's silence, the emerging events in the United States in mid-September 1957 caused Louis Armstrong—like Louis Jordan, seen as a genial jazzman by some and a grinning Uncle Tom by others—to finally snap.

"It's getting almost so bad, a colored man hasn't got any country," an exasperated Armstrong told a Grand Forks, North Dakota reporter. Armstrong railed that President Eisenhower had "no guts" and was "two-faced" and called Faubus "an uneducated plow boy"—with the reporter kindly substituting that term for publication rather than the more choice expletives that Armstrong actually called the Arkansas governor.

"The way they are treating my people in the South, the government can go to hell," Armstrong said. "The people over there [in other countries] ask me what's wrong with my country. What am I supposed to say?" he asked. "Don't get me wrong, the South is full of intelligent white people; it's bad for the lower-class people who make all the noise, though."

Armstrong then pulled out of an international goodwill tour of the Soviet Union planned by the U.S. State Department and, just in case someone missed his point, later added that he would rather play the Soviet Union than Arkansas, as long as Faubus remained in charge there. It was a spectacular outburst of political reality from a beloved American entertainer who, like Louie, was often accused of "Tomming."

Oddly, Armstrong was performing at Grand Forks's own Central High School at the time—and, in a further coincidence, Grand Forks was the hometown of Judge Ronald Davies, the judge who had ordered desegregation to proceed in Little Rock.

• •

"I'm a fella that wants to say, discrimination has gone its way," Louie sang in his recording of "Ofay and Oxford Gray," that rare 1940s song rejecting American racism. "So let's just smile and just be gay, there's no line." In the bridge, Louie explains that ofay "means white" and oxford "means colored they say," "if you're hip to the jive."

"Piano keys are black and white," he later notes, years before Michael Jackson and Paul McCartney's "Ebony and Ivory" hit, "they make the harmony."

Louie's typically prudent philosophy was to go along to get along: "All through the years going down South, I stayed where I was supposed to stay, dealt with all the people I was supposed to deal with, and I socialized with the people that I was supposed to socialize with, according to the racist rule…The white crackers, they appreciated that and when I went to deal with them, they'd say, 'You're Louis Jordan, aren't you?,' and I got better recognition from them. They did more for me than they would for someone else who was trying to lift themselves up before their time came."

Martha Jordan claims that Louie did more for civil rights than meets the eye:

> He demanded respect every place that he played, I know that, and every place that he went, he definitely did—from the [venue] owners and everybody else…I tell you what, he did that, a lot of people did not know.

When he went down south, say for instance, he and the band they would drive and go to certain hotels and motels and kept going through them, and going through them, and being rejected. And they went enough times going back and forth, 'til finally some of the hotels and motels [where] they would go through and were rejected, finally said, "OK, we're sick of losing this money." And they started letting them in. And a lot of people didn't know this, but that's how he would break it down.

In mid-1973, Louie reflected, "White kids are today much more open to black culture and the black experience than even the blacks—they're closed up…I don't want to be tolerated. If you give me a job and I can't do it, fire me and hire a white boy if he does a better job. Not just keep me there because I'm black."

"In many ways," said James Brown, "the entire civil rights movement began when a white kid in the audience stood up and cheered for a black performer."

· · · · · · · · · · · · · · · · · · · ·

Louie went to his next booking, two months at the Sands in Las Vegas, Nevada, in a melancholy mood.

A triumphant Arkansas homecoming had turned grim and things with Vicky were more often sour than not, while changing musical tastes—on which he had once ridden the crest of the wave—filled him with uncertainty.

Further, Louie was tiring of the expense and headaches of maintaining his band. He would soon disband, and then re-form again, his Tympany Five with various new and old members and also attempt working from a pool of musicians for gigs rather than hiring them full time before finally simply working as a solo performer.

Louie and the band returned to the Caribbean in 1958 to play a series of shows, again highlighting calypso numbers in the set. Gorgeous Dottie Smith—who'd joined the Tympany Five fold in August 1952—was also a hit. She would remain part of Louie's band for a decade, as other Tympany Five members came and went.

Louie had become dissatisfied with his decreasing bookings and finally left his longtime booking agency, GAC, where his one-time agent Berle Adams had risen from an office boy to being Louie's agent and parlayed that success into becoming an executive at MCA. Louie left GAC in 1959 to sign with Associated Booking Corporation. Associated Booking was run by Joe Glaser, Louis Armstrong's longtime manager.

Glaser had made his name parlaying some shadowy Chicago underworld connections into going legit with Armstrong after Prohibition ended. Glaser had helped get Armstrong on Decca, also Louie's label, in the mid-1930s. Glaser and Armstrong had worked together for more than a quarter century by the time Louie joined Associated Booking. Martha Jordan would later maintain that Glaser's allegiance to Armstrong—and the jealous thought that "another Louis" would supplant Armstrong in popularity—prevented Louie from getting choice bookings through Glaser's Associated agency: "I tell you what…[after] Joe Glaser…finally picked up Louie, I asked him once, 'Why are you making a million dollars off of Louis Armstrong and you don't put them together? They play different types of music—and you could make another million dollars off of Louis Jordan.' Which, he never answered me, but I thought it was completely out of the way and wrong. It looked like he was keeping…Louis Jordan out of Pops's way."

Whatever the case, Louie did not find his fortunes improving.

Chapter 12

"I DIDN'T WANT TO CHANGE MY STYLE"

Louie began the 1960s much like he had finished out the 1950s—with impatience over his lack of chart success and blame directed at the new sounds.

"We started it, but it's been changed," the musician who'd recently recorded such titles as "Rock 'n' Roll Call" and "Rock Doc" told a *Down Beat* interviewer regarding rock 'n' roll in the February 1960 issue.

"The music is bad, or the words are bad if the music is good," Louie said. In the article, Louie gives rock music "just about one year more."

In truth, by the time a year had passed, Louie had disbanded the Tympany Five, was without a recording contract and was working as a guest star with other groups, like that of trumpeter/vocalist Debby Hayes.

Furthermore, he and wife Vicky were splitting up, and Louie looked to leave Phoenix, where he had lived for years because the climate helped his arthritis. Louie ended up selling his house to religious leader Elijah Muhammad and relocating to Los Angeles.

Actually, Louie was on target about the state of rock 'n' roll at that time—Buddy Holly was dead, Chuck Berry was in jail, Little Richard had gotten religion and retired, Jerry Lee Lewis was in disgrace for marrying his teenaged cousin and Elvis Presley was in the army. But this rocking void would not be filled by Louis Jordan and his Tympany Five.

In March 1960, Louie was a featured performer on *Startime*, a live coast-to-coast TV broadcast sponsored by Ford Motor Company with emcee Ronald Reagan, subtitled *The Singing Years*. Louie and Reagan discussed the vagaries of the Apollo Theatre in some light scripted banter before Louie was called onstage. There, he backed Dinah Washington before performing a hot "Choo Choo Ch'Boogie." Despite such a high-profile nod, there was no doubt it was a nostalgia piece.

In 1961, Louie recorded a pair of singles for the Warwick label, which went nowhere—and they'd been his first releases in a while.

"A lot of companies have asked me to record," Louie alleged in a 1969 interview, "but they insisted that I go into rock 'n' roll, and I didn't want to change my style."

• • • • • • • • • • • • • • • • • • • •

In 1962, welcome news came to Louie from an unexpected source: an offer to record for Tangerine Record Corporation, Ray Charles's new label. Charles was an acolyte of Louie's music. He'd covered several Tympany Five songs such as "Let the Good Times Roll," "Choo Choo Ch'Boogie" and "Early in the Morning" and had a hit with "Don't Let the Sun Catch You Crying."

Charles's first national hit, "I Got a Woman," came in 1955, combining gospel and R&B. By 1962, again successfully melding musical styles with his *Modern Sounds in Country & Western Music* album, Charles's star had risen to the point where he rated his own label.

In contrast, the years with Louie ice-cold on the charts were adding up.

Louie's Tangerine sessions featured the big band that recorded with Charles, with most of the arrangements by ace Ernie Freeman. Several singles and an album called *Hallelujah...Louis Jordan Is Back!* were subsequently issued, the actual record labels of which were indeed tangerine-colored. Unlike his post-Decca low points, Louie wasn't just re-doing his hits here, save for "Saturday Night Fish Fry" and "Coleslaw," an obscurity originally recorded in 1949, which extols the benefits of the raw cabbage dish as served in his home state.

Additionally, he accessed material written by some of the greats of the new generation of blues and R&B performers: Floyd Dixon ("Never Know When a Woman Changes Her Mind"), Eddie Curtis ("Hard Head") and Titus Turner ("Workin' Man"), among others. "Hard Head" became a particular concert favorite.

Louie also audaciously covered "What'd I Say," which had become Charles's first million-selling single just three years before. Charles's well-rehearsed big band sounds wonderfully full behind Louie's ever-versatile singing.

"Old Age," another Tangerine single, aims to cheer "all you young people over forty" with its refrain, "Don't let a few years change your mind/Old age

Louis Jordan had high hopes for a comeback with 1964's *Hallelujah...Louis Jordan Is Back!* on the label owned by Jordan influence Ray Charles. *Courtesy Old State House Museum.*

ain't nothing but a matter of time." With a song like this—not to mention Louie being in his mid-fifties—the youth market wasn't being targeted this go-round.

Although Louie was happy with the music from the Tangerine sessions, he became decidedly displeased with the music's distribution, which was handled by Charles's home record label, ABC-Paramount. At the time, ABC-Paramount was a huge conglomerate with all the international television and film clout its two corporate names implied but with little experience in the music business—which may or may not fully explain the material's absence from the marketplace. Louie told of bringing copies to disc jockeys himself and taking the albums to sell at shows while on tour with Moms Mabley. Even years later, Louie complained to interviewers that DJs had played the Tangerine material but fans could not find the records in stores.

Other notables on Tangerine include Percy Mayfield, who wrote Charles's smash "Hit the Road Jack"; Ike and Tina Turner; the Ohio Players; and Charles's female singers, the Raelettes. Louie's affiliation with Tangerine Records ended in 1964. Tangerine folded when Charles left ABC-Paramount in 1973.

Louie's Tangerine catalogue remains the most glaring unreleased item in his discography—and indeed, at this writing, no Tangerine album ever has been officially reissued.

"I think he must have signed me up as a tax deduction or something," Louie said of Charles. Martha agreed that Louie could never understand why Charles in their eyes did not push the *Hallelujah* record, especially after being so aggressive in getting him to sign to Tangerine. "Ray Charles *begged* Louie to sign with his label…I thought it was utterly ridiculous," she said.

Strangely, Charles would generally acknowledge Louie's influence: "He was such a great showman, with a sense of humor and an unforgettable tongue-in-cheek style, that, after hearing him once, I couldn't forget him, and I became a great fan. His mastery of the alto saxophone impressed me so much that people tell me that my own alto sax style in some ways resembles his."

An oft-repeated quote from Charles regarding Louie does seem laced with a qualifier or two: "I have to admit that Louis Jordan has had a great and lasting influence upon my appreciation of music and, perhaps, even my performance."

"I'll go to my grave thinking it was ridiculous," Martha says of the sour Tangerine experience.

"I have never cared for Ray Charles because of that."

Chapter 13

"LET'S DON'T TALK ABOUT THE WINTERS"

On June 15, 1962, Jim Jordan died in Brinkley of a heart attack, a day shy of his birthday.

Even midway through his eighth decade, Jim had stayed active and interested in music and was part-time caretaker of the Haven of Rest cemetery. Fearing for his safety, Louie had scolded his dad for riding a bicycle around Brinkley. Jim Jordan had steered Louie toward music, and the rewards reaped from the seeds that Jim planted were more than either had dared to dream.

Jim had been a constant for Louie throughout his life, and although as a working musician Jim wasn't always around for young Louie, he'd always seen to it that someone was available to approximate a family for his son. As an adult, Louie helped take care of his dad financially even as Louie, in turn, was on the road and unable to come back home very often or for very long. Typically, Louie didn't dwell on his loss and was soon back at work.

Louie still didn't employ a full-time Tympany Five but instead continued working as a guest star with preexisting or assembled bands. Thus, when Louie, at age fifty-four, finally got the chance to tour England that winter, he went by himself—no entourage, no Tympany Five, not even a traveling companion. He was scheduled to play with trombonist Chris Barber and his band, with featured female vocalist Ottilie Patterson. Barber made a laudable side career in bringing over American performers, including Rosetta Tharpe, and touring and recording with them, and Barber and band were well regarded in Britain in their own right.

Bad weather diverted Louie's London-bound plane to Prestwick, Scotland, resulting in delays, in Louie catching a cold and in the cancellation of the opening tour dates. But once he and the band did play, they were a sensation to crowds, and Louie was a revelation to his fellow players as they performed through Sheffield, Bristol and Croydon. He and the band did the *Saturday Club* radio show for the BBC in London and recorded an album with the Barber band. Louie, Barber and the band reworked T5 classics like "Is You Is or Is You Ain't (My Baby)," "Choo Choo Ch'Boogie," "Don't Worry 'Bout That Mule" and "I'm Gonna Move to the Outskirts of Town," as well as also-rans like "A Man Ain't a Man" and "No Chance Blues" and evergreens like "I Wish I Could Shimmy Like My Sister Kate" and "Indiana."

Most intriguingly, they re-recorded "Fifty Cents," which Louie had done as a single for Warwick Records but had subsequently disappeared from the marketplace. The biggest difference the Barber band adds is Eddie Smith's banjo, which brings a Dixieland flavor to the mix. Louie admired Smith's banjo playing and told the band he'd plucked around on a banjo in his Arkansas youth—and also once knew a girl named Ottilie.

Meanwhile, Louie had long since gotten reacquainted with old flame Martha Weaver, typically even as he and Vicky were still together. The adopted biracial daughter of a black dentist and his wife, Martha grew up in privilege in a nice neighborhood in St. Louis, Missouri, but chose the life of a dancer and chorus girl. Hence, Louie's nickname for her: "the debutante who went astray." They'd actually met many years prior when Martha was still a teenager already interested in dance. Louie had come to St. Louis for a show at Kiel Auditorium, and a local young chorus line was being used from an annual high school revue that Martha had participated in called the "Y Circus." When Louie and Martha met at the auditorium, Louie realized that Martha's father, Memphis native Dr. Chalmers Weaver, had previously done dental work for him and that Louie had even eaten at Martha's home.

"By this time in my life," Martha says, "I had already met many other celebrities, several of whom became my personal friends. Even though I was impressed, I probably wasn't that excited because meeting and working with celebrities had become the norm for me...I probably would have been quite a bit more impressed if I had any idea that he, the jazz great Louis Jordan, would one day be my husband."

After rehearsals for the show, the two would meet for drinks, and Louie then asked his new young acquaintance—whom he occasionally called "Bud"—to come with him to his next stop, Atlantic City, New Jersey. She did, staying a week.

Louis Jordan and St. Louis, Missouri native Martha Weaver married in 1966 after several years together.

"I discovered Louis Jordan was a very unique person," Martha says. "He shared some very confidential information about his personal life with me. He said that he was with his second wife then. He also talked about Fleecie, whom I found out was his first wife." (Martha has maintained that she is Louie's third, not fifth, wife and disputes the legitimacy of Louie's matrimony with both Julia and Ida.)

Their paths crossed for some time, often when Martha was a chorus girl at the Apollo in New York City. The relationship continued sporadically before it finally became serious. (Martha's other romantic encounters included Louis Armstrong, Sammy Davis Jr. and Nat Cole.) Martha says she and her mother shared an apartment with Louie in Los Angeles for four years until he was able to obtain his divorce from Vicky.

Louie and Martha married on June 14, 1966. He had to leave the next day to perform, so they waited until the next month for the wedding reception, held at a Los Angeles hotel.

"Most all of the chorus girls I had worked with over the years had gotten married long before I did," she says. "Louie and I surprised everyone when we tied the knot because we were always so on-again, off-again with our relationship."

Literally and figuratively, Martha became part of Louie's act.

Louie appeared on *The !!!! Beat Show* in 1966, a regional American television show specializing in R&B and soul music acts. The program was

A lifelong musician, Louis Jordan continued to perform
enthusiastically into his sixties, years after he'd had a hit single.

hosted by WLAC-Nashville disc jockey Bill "Hoss" Allen. In one episode,
Louie is backed by the show's house band, the Beat Boys, featuring Clarence
"Gatemouth" Brown, doing a fast and loose "Saturday Night Fish Fry,"
complete with a pair of go-go dancers. Allen makes a couple of cracks about
Louie's longevity in the business until finally Louie retorts, "Let's don't talk
about the winters—talk about the summers." "All right, baby, you're all right
with me," Allen laughs in retreat.

In another hot segment for the show with his own band, Louie and his
Tympany Five (actually four here) blow through an uptempo instrumental
in which every piece gets a solo turn, including once-former Tympany Five
drummer Joe "Christopher Columbus" Morris, who had come back to play
with Louie after many years and now called himself "Chris Columbo."
Guitarist Leo Belvin, keyboardist Kenny Andrews (playing a Hammond
B-3) and Napoleon Fuller on tenor sax filled out the Tympany Five. Then
in his late fifties, Louie led the group on a thunderous rampage, with all
showing their stuff in less than a minute.

The rave-up had been preceded by an interesting instrumental choice;
Louie gives a nod to Tympany Five sideman-turned-star Bill Doggett by
doing Doggett's "Ram-Bunk-Shush," a hit from a decade before. Dressed

in a black sequined gown, Martha busts a few go-go moves before sashaying off-camera. Louie and the band recognize a new generation of war troops, this time in Vietnam, by dusting off "G.I. Jive."

Louie and Martha duet on "All I Do Is Dream," and the Tympany Five warhorses "Don't Let the Sun Catch You Crying" and "Caldonia Boogie" are also aired. Louie tries out a new opening couplet with some hip modern lingo—"I got a baby with a crazy pad—woo! She makes me so mad!" Even after all these years, "Caldonia" wouldn't be complete without some light footwork and synchronized kicks by Louie, Belvin and Fuller. After his high kick during the song's break, Louie marks the air where his foot had reached, which was around eye level, as if to note, "Not bad."

The pair of episodes, one solo and one with the Tympany Five, on this regional, now obscure program was apparently Louie's only color American television appearances.

Through the decade, Louie's health became a concern. He'd had hernia problems since he was a youth, and Tympany Five audiences might have been stunned to know that the bandleader doing all the high kicks was often wearing a truss. He'd also had heart trouble. James Brown recalls finally meeting his idol Louis Jordan, whom he had previously only seen in Soundies and movies, at the Apollo Theater in New York.

"I stayed over for a day to see him. It was the first time I'd ever watched him live. He was a very sick man, but he still put on a great show. Afterward, I got a chance to talk with him for a few minutes and told him what he'd meant to me as a performer," Brown said.

"He was a good man and still hasn't gotten his due."

Chapter 14

"THE GREATEST HITMAKER
OF ALL TIMES"

At the end of the 1960s, Louie undertook the route of many American entertainers at career valleys: goodwill U.S. military tours. Louie and Martha and band performed through Thailand, Korea, Taiwan, the Philippines and Japan, mostly playing U.S. Air Force bases, in 1967. They would do duets on songs like "Hello, Dolly" and old Louie and Ella numbers. Louie got reacquainted with pianist Maurice Rocco, who had relocated to Bangkok. He and Rocco were peers from back in the day and hadn't seen each other in twenty-five years. Louie did a return tour of the area in 1970.

Even better, Louie found himself on a newly formed jazz label, Pzazz. Its slogan: Put Some Pzazz in Your Jazz. Based in Hollywood, Pzazz Records was formed by Paul Gayten, born on January 29, 1920, in Kentwood, Louisiana. He and Louie had known each other for decades, and Gayten had his own influential connections to the modern sounds. At Chess Records, he'd produced such songs as "See You Later, Alligator" by Bobby Charles, "Ain't Got No Home" by Clarence "Frogman" Henry and "Carol" by Chuck Berry. As a writer, Gayten's own biggest song was "The Music Goes Round and Round." Gayten died on March 26, 1991.

Recording with a fourteen-piece orchestra, Louie got started with a couple of singles in the fall of 1968. A seasonal song, "Santa Claus, Santa Claus," got some attention but unfortunately wasn't released until nearly mid-December. Opening with a slowed-down "Jingle Bells" riff, "Santa Claus, Santa Claus" then segues into an uptown blues lament, with Louie waiting for St. Nick to deliver his loved one.

This 1968 album is confusingly titled *One-Sided Love, Then Sakatumi*. In the liner notes, Sammy Davis Jr. calls Louis Jordan the "Original Soul Brother." *Courtesy Ken DelVecchio.*

Another Pzazz single, "New Orleans and a Rusty Old Horn," also got some radio play and became a latter-day concert favorite for Louie—he often pointed to the song as a strong example of his post–Decca Records period. And Louie's hot version of the instrumental song "Bullitt" surpasses the one found on the 1968 *Bullitt* original film soundtrack by Lalo Schrifin. An incredible sax trill at the end of the number showcases Louie's long-developed breath control.

Somewhat confusingly, the Pzazz album is called *One-Sided Love, Then Sakatumi*, in apparent reference to the opening songs on either side of the disc. Four of the eleven album tracks were written by Jackson, Mississippi native Teddy Edwards, who was also the main of the album's three musical arrangers. Jack Scott arranged "Watch the World" and "I'll Get Along Somehow," while Carroll Skinner arranged "New Orleans and a Rusty Old Horn" and "Sakatumi."

"The A-Men Corner," an Edwards number on religious sanctimony and hypocrisy—kind of a grown-up "Deacon Jones"—closes the record.

On the front cover of the Pzazz LP, Martha and Louie are both dressed in traditional Asian garb in apparent reference to the song "Sakatumi," souvenirs of Louie's recent tours through Asia. You can hear some of Louie and Martha's stage banter and routines on songs like "I'll Get Along Somehow." But in terms of album sales, none of the effort did much good. "Santa Claus, Santa Claus" became the song with the most interest, but its release was tardy, and because of its seasonal nature, the song wasn't even included on the album.

Despite a few sub-par or ill-fitting song choices, Louie sounds confident and relaxed throughout the Pzazz album. And, like his efforts for Tangerine, Louie demonstrates he's still in full possession of his talents. Sadly, as with Louie's Tangerine releases, only the most ardent fan was able to find the album or the singles.

Sammy Davis Jr. wrote the Pzazz album liner notes: "Louis Jordan (possibly the greatest hit maker of all times [*sic*]) was the first recording artist to project basic Negro life and Situations (Life and Situations of the Black Community, if you prefer) on records with humor and dignity. I and many others like me have dropped nickel after nickel in the juke box to enjoy his messages in song and monologue."

Davis then mentions some high-profile Tympany Five titles, adding, "Well, Chillun, in case you weren't around, you missed some goodies. In fact, some of the above-mentioned [songs] set the pattern for several of our present day performers."

Oddly, Davis didn't mention it in his otherwise effusive liner notes, but he got some of his first breaks in the music business as an opening act for Louie when Davis was dancing with the Will Mastin Trio. Davis does in his liner notes acknowledge Louie as "the Original Soul Brother." While not mentioning James Brown by name, and "all due respect to some of those that make this claim [of the title 'Soul Brother Number One'] or have it thrust upon them. But as far back as I can remember the man in question (Mr. LOUIS JORDAN) is the Original Soul Brother."

Martha had been romantically involved with Davis at one time and, in her 2005 memoir, says Davis asked her to marry him in 1951, but she said no. More understandably, Davis doesn't mention any of that in his liner notes, either. Martha said she and Davis met at the Club Harlem in Atlantic City, New Jersey ("definitely a segregated city," she adds), and the pair became an item back when Martha was a dancer and working with Joe "Ziggy" Johnson.

"After that," she says, "whenever Sammy and I were performing in the same city, we would always spend time being romantically involved with each other."

She also became friendly with Davis's mother, Baby Sanchez, who worked across the street from Club Harlem as a barmaid at the Little Belmont Club. Not yet a big name, Davis worked with the Will Mastin Trio and with Dean Martin and Jerry Lewis at Atlantic City's 500 Club.

"My relationship with Sammy was somewhat similar to my relationship with Louis Jordan," Martha says. "We would get together in whatever city we happened to be in at the same time. Sammy and I were good buddies, but Louie and I were actually in love. I knew that Sammy's feelings for me were really strong. I really liked him so much, but those feelings of love weren't mutual. They were for Louie, but he wasn't available for me like Sammy was," she says.

"Later in life when I was living in California, I had regrets that I didn't go to Vegas with Sammy to become his wife because I found out, through the chorus line grapevine, that he had to marry a black woman."

With all that, Martha still said in an interview with your author, "Louis was jealous of Sammy—why, I don't know."

(Martha, however, says there was no jealousy between Louie and Louis Armstrong: "Louis Armstrong and I were going out before Louis Jordan and I. Pops and I just sorta got together with one another, but it wasn't a permanent thing, because Pops was married. Everybody knew Pops, you know.")

• • • • • • • • • • • • • • • • • • •

Most striking is how little of Louie's own sax playing is on *One-Sided Love, Then Sakatumi*. Gayten announced that would be rectified on the next Jordan Pzazz album, which he said would have more of a stripped-down, Tympany Five feel but with electric bass instead of stand-up bass "and some of the contemporary combo feeling."

As for the material, Jordan said, "We're going to do a blues album. I've never had a blues album—would you believe it? Here I've been associated with the blues all my life, but the whole time I was with Decca, they were so busy making money with my singles that they never thought about albums, so I missed out on that chance."

Note the subtle dig at his former recording company—though Decca had technically released an album of Louie's songs during his time with the company, the collection of four of his 78 rpm singles in 1946, and would eventually release many more.

"A heavy proportion of my big things were based on the blues changes," Louie acknowledged, although despite his Mississippi River Delta birthright, his general take on blues was certainly not Delta-style.

At the time of the release, Louie also unwittingly sounded like a musician uncertain of his artistic path—which he surely must have been, with a second decade in the commercial wilderness coming to an end: "I want to do some numbers in my regular blues style, but I don't think there's any reason not to adjust myself to what's happening right now. I might sing a couple of tunes the way kids are doing them today."

"But essentially," Louie says, again surmising that changing his style must be key to his future success, "I think the music is going to make the difference—my updating some of the songs I did before, modernizing the arrangements."

Despite Gayten's efforts, Louie's album didn't take off, nor did any of the label's other output. Louie later complained that the three different musical arrangers on the album each wanted him to sing a different way. "They wouldn't let me sing like I wanted to sing," Louie said.

"That's not the way to treat an artist—so it wasn't really successful."

Would Louie have been more circumspect in his complaints had the album been a hit? The proposed second Jordan Pzazz blues-oriented album with a modern Tympany Five sound—something that with benefit of hindsight sounds tantalizing musically as well as commercially—was never made. Gayten retired in the 1970s, and Pzazz Records folded.

Somewhere along the line, Louie had become a man who had outlived his musical moment.

Chapter 15

"WHY SHOULD SO TALENTED AN ARTIST REMAIN THE ROCHESTER OF THE JAZZ ENTERTAINER?"

It wasn't as if Louie had the luxury not to work. Martha laughs, "He knew I wasn't with him for his money!

"Louie was not the millionaire that I knew he once had been," Martha explained. "Let's put it like this—he was a millionaire *before* I met him. He had some wives that just didn't take care of him and his money. And Uncle Sam didn't either. And the people that were looking out for him didn't—his managers and things."

She said, "I learned that so much happened to Louie in his life that was negative. When I think back about it, it really was pitiful that he was on the losing end of so many deals that fell through. He trusted his wife, or someone else, to take care of the business for him, and they let him down numerous times."

In another part of the country—Chicago, Illinois—ex-wife Fleecie Moore was keeping in her family tradition of doing well financially with her property and with a generous regular subsidy, thanks to the publishing income she had on several of the most popular Tympany Five songs.

When he wasn't on the road, Louie enjoyed relaxing and entertaining around his swimming pool with his wife, who loved to swim and socialize. The couple had many friends and entertained a lot, especially Martha and her girlfriends. When bookings became lighter, Louie found—or returned to—other interests. He loved photography and even developed his own photos. When not taking pictures, he went fishing a lot, golfed, kept up with pro sports and bought a guitar and a drum set to bang around on.

He developed an interest in professional American football, particularly the Dallas Cowboys and the Los Angeles Rams. Martha had grown up Catholic, and Louie, who had grown up Baptist, would sometimes attend Mass with her on Sundays.

Louie continued his voracious reading habits—though more often of magazines rather than books. "So many people thought Louis Jordan was the type of person you saw onstage, as a comedian, or funny," Martha Jordan says. "But he was not. He was a very serious person." Louie was never the life of the party or even very talkative, Martha notes, but liked being able to hold court on current events at cocktail parties and get-togethers—when he wasn't having one of his quiet spells.

"He wasn't that type of person," she says. "He wasn't a 'hanger-outer' person like that. We would go out and have fun and do what we want to do, but he was not a hanger-outer. He was a very, very quiet person offstage. My husband was very respectful with everybody. Really, he was. Photography—and fishing, that was his main thing. If you got into a conversation with Louis Jordan, you would have thought he was a professor, or something like that. You would never have thought he was a musician, or in show business."

Louie's next recordings were with Johnny Otis, who had recently launched Blues Spectrum, a record label featuring the golden greats of rhythm and blues—and there was little doubt at this point that Louie belonged in this category. Otis was born John Veliotes in Vallejo, California, in 1921. He'd already made his name as a bandleader, DJ, TV show host, club owner, civil rights activist and hit-making producer before trying his hand at owning a record label. Other Blues Spectrum releases were by performers generally in the same demographic (and chart predicament) as Louie and included Big Joe Turner, Joe Liggins, Charles Brown, Connie "Pee Wee" Crayton (Louie had recorded her "I've Found My Peace of Mind" for Mercury in 1957) and Otis himself. But none on the roster had ridden so high, and fallen so far, as Louie.

Louie and Otis recorded in Los Angeles, California. "I owe my first trip to New York's legendary Apollo Theatre to Louis Jordan," Otis wrote in the liner notes to Louie's album. "In 1946, Louis took my band along as second on his bill. But before we could get to New York, I found myself stranded in Detroit with no money and fifteen musicians looking to me to solve the dilemma. Louis bailed me out with a cash loan and we were able to make the Apollo date and move on from there." Otis also recalled that whenever his band played shows with Louie in the late 1940s and early 1950s, "all the members of my group would stand in the wings and watch the master

This 1973 album for Johnny Otis's Blues Spectrum, including several Tympany Five–era retreads, leaves little doubt where Jordan stood with listeners.

showman at work. This was not a show of appreciation for any personal favors, however, this was a tribute to his compelling artistry."

Otis plays drums on the album. Once again, song preference is given to what had long since become Tympany Five classics, albeit ones now fading from memory: "Choo Choo Ch'Boogie," "Let the Good Times Roll," "Saturday Night Fish Fry," a slightly somber "Ain't Nobody Here But Us Chickens" and what are simply called "Outskirts of Town" and "Caldonia" in the notes. Otis's son Shuggie—forty-five years Louie's junior—played guitar, bass, piano and organ, while Irv Cox (tenor sax) and Bob Mitchell (trumpet) came in from the Tympany Five fold to fill out the sound.

The Blues Spectrum rearrangements of Tympany Five chestnuts in general fare better than usual thanks to the sympathetic treatment of the Otises. "Choo Choo Ch'Boogie," "Saturday Night Fish Fry" and "Caldonia" all receive faithful reinterpretations. Shuggie Otis shows an amazing capacity to mimic some of the tight musical flourishes that took the Tympany Five material from good to sublime million-sellers.

But as usual, most interesting are the new songs: "Helping Hand," a wonderful bit of hopeful Sanford and Townsend seventies-style sentiment ("Go find the people who are lost and give them a helping hand...do for them what you can") that was a far cry from Louie's hedonistic party-song persona. Days after he'd cut the song in the summer of 1973, he enthusiastically described it, saying, "It's got some very deep words, written by two white boys. It deals with a rundown woman sitting on her ghetto steps, watching her kids play, wondering if the Lord would take the time to hear her nightly prayer. It went on about the older kids, playing in the street, as she wondered if she'd have money to put shoes on all their feet. Now, see how deep that thinking is? And this is by two young kids, whipper-snappers, as you'd call them. But they're thinking and they're writing. It's not race or creed. It's the way they think." "Helping Hand" references homelessness, poverty and the prison population. Also, despite Louie's Christian upbringing, it is one of the surprisingly few of his songs with a reference to prayer or religiosity. This, coupled with its socially aware lyrics, finds "Helping Hand" standing lonely in Louie's canon.

The blues amalgam credited to the Otises, "I Got the Walkin' Blues," has Louie riffing against Shuggie's Elmore James–styled slide guitar.

On his recording of Damita Jo's "I'm a Good Thing," Louie could almost be speaking to his old fans: "I'm a good thing—can't you recognize?...I'm not sweet sixteen...I don't play hard to get, and what you get is as good as gold...that's what I've been told."

Louie's alto sax playing remained fluid, if his range a bit diminished, and his vocals remained flexible, if a bit raspier. And as usual, he sounds like he's having a really good time. But by this time, expectations for chart action had dimmed.

In July 1973, Louie—along with the likes of Earl "Fatha" Hines, Gene Krupa and Louie's old flame Ella Fitzgerald—returned to New York City to participate in the dedication of the former Singer Bowl in Queens, New York, as it was renamed the Louis Armstrong Memorial Stadium. Louie had also been asked to join in a reunion concert of the old Chick Webb Orchestra, to which he heartily agreed. He and the Tympany Five were subsequently given their own featured slot on the program and blew everyone away. He hadn't been a marquee name in New York City for years, and it had been even longer than that since he'd charted a hit in the region. East Coast tastemakers had forgotten the force of Louie's talent. "Two days short of his 65th birthday, Jordan sang and played like a man possessed, not content to remain a footnote in the histories of both jazz and rock," reported *Melody Maker* magazine.

The same year, bluesman Clarence "Gatemouth" Brown recorded the first Jordan tribute album: *"Gatemouth" Brown Sings Louis Jordan*. Louie and Brown had played together on TV in 1966 on *The !!!! Beat Show*, when Louie appeared and the latter led the house band.

Louie toured with the Pointer Sisters, where he was well received but was replaced with a ventriloquist act. In keeping with the mellower outlook he'd gained in maturity, he took the news in stride.

Louie played around the Los Angeles area that spring and summer. Leonard Feather reviewed Louie's two-week run at the Fire and Flame in Studio City: "Every song was at least 25 years old…Why should so talented an artist remain the Rochester of the jazz entertainer when he could be the Flip Wilson? Some fresh, hip material might enable him to relate to countless young hands." Louie had also been the recent subject of a "Where Are They Now?" piece in *Ebony* magazine.

Tom Arnold was Louie's drummer at the Fire and Flame club residency. He'd been noticed by Louie's tenor man Irv Cox (who would soon gain fame soloing on Jefferson Starship's 1975 hit "Miracles") playing at a jazz club in Virginia City, Nevada. Cox and the band were playing at Lake Tahoe. "I knew that Louie was really famous, but I didn't know much about the music," Arnold said. "I was weaned on the Doors, the Stones—rock 'n' roll."

Following an audition in Tahoe, Arnold was asked to join the group, but only after he completed a tutorial with the master. Newlyweds Arnold and his wife relocated to Los Angeles. However, she stayed in a different part of the city, at Louie's request. "He wanted me to stay at his place and concentrate on nothing but music every day," Arnold explains.

"So he didn't want me to see my wife—and I never did. The only time I left his house was to go to the market. On the other hand, I figured it was a very wonderful opportunity."

Arnold lived with Louie and Martha for nearly a month, working with Louie eight to ten hours a day. "There was nothing easy about it. He had a certain groove pattern that he needed to meet. He had some specialized ways of doing his shuffle."

Once Arnold finally made it onstage, he and the band did the Four Tops' current hit, "Ain't No Woman Like the One I Got" and 1972's "I Believe in Music" in addition to T5 classics. "[Louie] did do some standards, but not many. He mostly stuck to his own thing. He liked to do 'Knock Me a Kiss.' He did do 'Moon River,' but he did it in $^4/_4$ time and as a shuffle, which was interesting. He did 'Take the A Train.' He did 'C Jam Blues.'"

"Louie had a tremendous amount of stage energy. I'd never seen anybody entertain quite the way that he did. He was funny, yet classy, and he had a projection that very few musicians that I've ever seen had. Louie had that charisma. It went beyond the music—you just kind of liked to look at him," Arnold said.

As they played Los Angeles and Hawaii, Arnold "tried to approach these rhythms to where [Louie] was happy with them. He was so in tune with the drums from having such great drummers and working with the best." But Louie changed bass players and piano players during Arnold's brief tenure, and sure enough, drummer Archie Taylor—not Arnold—went with the band to Europe that fall.

"I really am still today experiencing the gravity of the situation [of playing with Louie]," Arnold said.

"It didn't really sink in until maybe years afterwards. And I didn't realize how big he was until years afterwards, the true weight of what he did, and to realize what an influence he really did have."

In November 1973, Louie went to Europe to play the Berlin Jazz Festival and other dates on the continent. Martha didn't go. After sharing the festival bill with names like Duke Ellington and Miles Davis, Louie performed in Sweden, Denmark and France, though beyond the German festival, the shows were hastily arranged.

While in Paris, Louie cut what would be his final album, *I Believe in Music*, issued on France's Black and Blue label. Here, we find the stern musical taskmaster at his most relaxed. The title track, a recent pop hit, shows the cabaret material Louie had been doing, which could include such Top 40 songs as "Help Me Make It Through the Night" and even the Beatles' "Hey Jude."

Opposite, top: Look out! Louis Jordan was an energetic performer throughout his career and proud of his high kicks.

Opposite, bottom: As Louis Jordan sang in the 1960s, "Don't let a few years change your mind / Old age ain't nothing but a matter of time."

For a man who had spent years perfecting the sound of a party on wax, Louie sounds like he is actually having a good time—possibly because the pressure to make a hit had finally receded. While several of the classic Tympany Five hits like "Saturday Night Fish Fry," "Is You Is or Is You Ain't (My Baby)," "Caldonia" and "I'm Gonna Move to the Outskirts of Town" are given the re-recording treatment, here it seems more for fun than duty. Lesser-known Decca tracks "It's a Low Down Dirty Shame" and "Three-Handed Woman" and tunes firmly in the Tympany Five vein, "Hard Head" (also done for Tangerine) and "Every Knock Is a Boost," were also recorded.

The tightly wound arrangements of the Tympany Five give way to a looser feel. "Outskirts" even clocks in at over six minutes. For the session, Louie had Irv Cox on tenor sax, Duke Burrell on piano and Archie Taylor on drums. John Duke, an American living in France, took over on bass when band member Louis Kabok broke his arm just before the trip. When *I Believe in Music* was reissued in 1992, a half dozen instrumental tracks Louie recorded the same day with Fred Below on drums, Louis Myers on guitar and Dave Myers on bass were included.

The relaxed nature of the recordings is notable, but the tantalizing fact is that while Louie sounds so good, he wouldn't record as a solo artist again.

Chapter 16

"HE FELT BETTER THAN HE'D FELT IN A LONG TIME"

In the spring of 1974, Louie began a months-long residency at the Marriott Hotel in New Orleans, Louisiana. Martha joined him later. "Despite the hokey, tourist-oriented revue concocted for him," *Living Blues* reported of the arrangement, "Jordan was still a warm, lively entertainer, singing, playing and jiving much the same as he did in the '40s." In addition to doing his gig, Louie attended the New Orleans Jazz and Heritage Festival and enjoyed the city. He also made what would be his last recordings.

Wallace Davenport, a trumpeter and owner of the My Jazz label, asked Louie to record as a sideman on Davenport's album, *Sweet Georgia Brown*. Louie also performed on the Pontchartrain gospel label release *I Shall Not Be Moved* by Sister Aline White in August.

He then took the rest of the summer off. As Martha says, "This presented a perfect opportunity for us to promote the Louis Jordan Golf Tournament. He planned to semi-retire after this trip and not be on the road so much, so he could play more golf."

She and Louie spent some time in Jamaica. Martha had been noticing that Louie kept saying he was tired, even when he rested all day. "This was very unlike Louie, because he loved the sun, the pool and the beauty of the outdoors. He loved to take pictures all the time and he was missing some great photo opportunities because of his tiredness. I kept checking on him all the time, but he said he was OK."

In September 1974, Louie went to the Reno, Nevada area to work at the Golden Nugget Casino in Sparks. Martha stayed in Los Angeles for her job as office manager of an elementary school, which she had taken in anticipation of Louie's semi-retirement, and she was preparing to go to night school. Louie had been at the engagement for less than a week when she got the call that he had suffered a heart attack. He was in intensive care at St. Mary's Hospital in Reno for three weeks before he was able to come back to California. Louie would never fully recover.

It was a grim holiday season for the Jordans. Louie was told not to exert himself—much less play the saxophone. Unfortunately, it seemed he was finally getting some good bookings again. He was set to return to Europe to appear at the Nice Jazz Festival in July, and other booking agents didn't seem to mind that he could only sing, not play the saxophone.

But Louie didn't make it that far.

One afternoon in early February, after he and Martha had been out to see about her attending night school, he told her that he was tired and was going to take a nap. He sat down on the bed but lost consciousness, rolled onto the floor and never got up. It was February 4, 1975.

That morning, Louie had told Martha that he felt better than he'd felt in a long time. Martha said later she should have recognized that statement as a red flag—her mother had told her the same thing on the day she died.

Louie's funeral service was held in Los Angeles at Spalding La Brea Chapel. Lou Rawls sang "Just a Closer Walk with Thee," while saxist Irv Cox performed an instrumental take on "Is You Is or Is You Ain't (My Baby)."

Louie's former manager, Berle Adams—by then CEO of Universal-MCA—was among the attendees and recalled, "All in attendance placed a plastic saxophone on his casket as they left the funeral parlor. The minister's eulogy was unusual and effective; he built his remarks around the titles of Louie's hit records, using them to tell the story of Louie's life and times."

President Gerald Ford sent his formal condolences, which were read at the service.

Louie was interred not in Brinkley in his home state of Arkansas but at Mt. Olive Cemetery in the Lemay suburb of Martha's hometown of St. Louis, Missouri, as he had requested. There's a spot for Martha, and already buried in adjacent plots are her parents—Dr. Chalmers Weaver and Eliza Weaver, a native of Webster Groves, Missouri, also a suburb of St. Louis. The *St. Louis Argus*, one of the city's black newspapers, reported Louie's death on its front page, above the fold.

"He was my heart. He was my life, he really was. Cause he's been dead thirty-something years, and I haven't gotten over it, really," Martha says.

"When Louie passed away, I lost my lover, companion, best friend and my husband, whom I loved more than life itself," she says. "It took me almost two years to get myself together enough to get out of the house and away from Los Angeles."

Chapter 17

"IT IS ABSOLUTELY NOTHING NEW"

A long the way, MCA had acquired the rights to the extensive musical catalogue of Decca Records. That included the important seminal recordings of Louis Jordan (as well as those of Ella Fitzgerald, with Milt Gabler behind most of the production of both). So the company that Berle Adams, Louie's longtime manager, helped steer into a behemoth would end up with control of Louie's most popular recordings, as well as the majority of his lifetime recorded output.

Over the years, the corporation hadn't done much with Louie's huge archive of music; some might even call it a neglect that is a key element to Louie's post-1950s lack of name recognition. The vast majority of the Louis Jordan Decca catalogue had remained out of print for decades, with a lone "Best Of" album featuring a couple of handfuls of Louie's greatest hits being the only legitimately released item available to American fans for years.

Joe Jackson's 1981 tribute album to Louie, *Jumpin' Jive*, helped revive Louie's name, particularly in the U.K., where Louie's records had remained somewhat popular, especially considering that he never toured there during his prime. In addition to such Tympany Five hits as "Five Guys Named Moe" and "Is You Is," Jackson and his six-piece band further display deep knowledge of their "main inspiration" Louie by covering lesser-known early Tympany Five numbers as "You're My Meat" and "You Run Your Mouth (And I'll Run My Business)."

In the liner notes, Jackson calls Louis "the king of jukeboxes, who influenced so many but is acknowledged by so few. Like us, he didn't aim at purists, or

With deep Louis Jordan tracks rarely heard at the time, this 1983 U.K. release promised it was "not another roundup of greatest hits." Posthumous Jordan fans were getting hipper to Jordan's jive.

even jazz fans—just anyone who wanted to listen and enjoy." The Jackson album is said to have helped create the swing dancing revival that grew in popularity in England and subsequently peaked in the United States in the late 1990s but continues on in pockets on both continents and beyond.

As for the irony of Louie being remembered, if at all, mainly for his funny party songs when he was a serious player and a quiet man, Martha is philosophical: "That was his gift—that he could do this. This was his gift as a show person. To do this type of song with a gimmick to them, like a fun thing. That was his gift, his way of portraying a song…Let me put it like this: These were the types of songs he started with, these were the types of songs he could sell, and these were the types of songs that people understood him to do. And they made money, they went over."

With no mention of the Tympany Five or any of its storied individual members, Louis Jordan was inducted into Cleveland, Ohio's Rock and Roll Hall of Fame in 1987. He was in the second "class" of inductees—some whom Louie had influenced, such as Ray Charles, had been inducted the previous inaugural year. Both Louie's hit-making and musical influence among rock and R&B legends made his selection into the hall obvious. That's not to mention his influence in jazz, pop, blues, rap, ska, reggae and even country music and his helping introduce calypso music to America and his groundbreaking work in what later was known as music video. But the induction was not without irony, considering Louie's aversion toward the rock genre, which helped usurp his King of the Jukeboxes crown.

And since the beat of America's rebellious youth must always change from its forebears, rap and hip-hop were the genres that supplanted rock and R&B music. There are few overt links that point toward Louis Jordan and the Tympany Five, with his shuffle rhythm being seemingly less compatible for sampling with the backbeat-heavy rhythms of hip-hop. The promising 1990s trend of jazz sampling by acts such as Digable Planets, Us3, trip-hopper Tricky and others concentrated mainly in modern postwar jazz—and did not take in the long haul. Still, many influenced by Louie, perhaps most prolifically the beats of James Brown songs, have had their songs repurposed through sampling.

Down to the pencil-thin moustache and tailored suits, Morris Day with his valet Jerome and band the Time particularly ran with the self-absorbed would-be womanizer dandy persona in the 1980s and 1990s, with Kanye West and Andre "3000" Benjamin picking up the mantle in the late 1990s and early 2000s. Snoop Dogg, Cypress Hill, Ludacris and countless other rappers and acts have also had their various takes on the humorous drunken/ stoned hipster, with a generous side of misogyny and relationship issues, in their images and songs. It was territory that Louis Jordan and the Tympany Five covered in songs like "Beware," "Look Out," "Saturday Night Fish Fry," "Open the Door, Richard," "Jordan for President," "Have You Got the Gumption?," "Hard Head" and many other titles.

"Louie used to talk his songs, but he'd talk his songs and you knew what he was talking about. They're doing rap now, you don't know what the hell they're saying," Martha says, adding that she abhors the genre's "vulgarity," as would Louie: "He would never have cursed in any of his shows or any of his numbers, because of the young people."

Martha says, "He did all these [songs with Louie 'rapping'] years ago, because they were selling. So this is nothing new to me now—what they're doing, the rap and stuff—it is absolutely nothing new."

For decades, illegal bootlegs—like this undated European release—expensive imports or vintage 78s were the only means for most listeners to hear anything beyond a handful of Louis Jordan's greatest hits.

Endless rehearsals, matching suits, dance moves and song routines made the band, but it was Louie's brand of sophisticated yet down-home jump blues and vocals that was the singular force behind the whirlwind. The small size of his Tympany Five made it innovative structurally and musically during the big band era. Among the first to join electric guitar and bass with horns, Louie set the framework for decades of future R&B and rock combos. His rapid rhymes are a precursor to rap, his beats a precursor to hip-hop. Louie's a direct link from the American minstrel show tradition as he continues to influence evolving branches of pop, rock, jazz, blues, rap and more. Rhythm

& blues and rock, in addition to post–World War II jazz and blues, would be very different if not for the music of Louis Jordan and his Tympany Five. Louie directly influenced those we've long considered to be *the* primary rock, R&B, blues and jazz influences themselves: Chuck Berry, James Brown, Ray Charles, B.B. King, Bo Diddley, Little Richard, Freddie King, Sonny Rollins and so many more. Thus, without Louis Jordan and his Tympany Five, there are no Beatles, no Rolling Stones, no Michael Jackson, no Prince.

Louie's innovative music spawned more than fifty top-ten hits. He not only had numerous number-one hits through the 1940s, but many would stay at the top for weeks at a time and topped the charts of other genres as well. In fact, for eight years through the 1940s, Jordan's records were so popular that his songs held the number one spot for a combined 113 weeks. That adds up to more than two years total with a Jordan song on top. His songs continue to be played and appear in countless commercials, TV shows, movies and beyond and have been recorded by hundreds of popular artists across the globe.

But somehow, the name Louis Jordan hasn't stuck. Never strictly a blues artist, and too pop for jazz and too jazz for pop, Louie was also too early to be considered an R&B or rock performer. Label-hopping, poor distribution and sometimes weak material marred his profile and record sales performance during the album era. Timing also saw Louie mostly sidestepping the American and European festival circuits, which saw the revival of many a performer's career, particularly in blues.

Instead of being embraced by all the variety of musical genres in which he's played a major part, Mr. Jordan ended up falling through most every single crack.

Ask his widow why the Louis Jordan name isn't better known, and she flippantly says, "Because he's dead! It's as simple as that!" She laughs and then thinks for a moment. "And everybody's not playing him." Martha said she tried to get her local Las Vegas radio stations to play Louie, to no avail.

"It's unreal, but I cannot give you the answer."

Chapter 18

"GOOD TIMES ROLL"

A musical revue of Tympany Five songs, *Five Guys Named Moe*, played on London's West End, New York's Broadway and throughout America in the 1990s. "I cried," Martha said upon seeing the play for the first time. "It was fantastic." She had hoped it would run longer on Broadway than two years but said she harbored no illusions that the musical would bring Louie's music back.

Though the *Five Guys* musical is often given a large role in spurring latter-day critical rethinking of Louie's music, the profile of Louis Jordan, as a man or musician, remains low throughout the play. Furthermore, music fans and writers in some quarters have been noting the need for such a reanalysis at least since the 1960s. Leonard Feather wrote in 1969 that Louie's "impact in the '40s was comparable to that of the Beatles in the '60s."

A stronger single item that broadened thought about Louis Jordan's place in American song was *Louis Jordan: Let the Good Times Roll*, a nine-CD retrospective released by Germany's Bear Family Records in 1992, collecting Louie's entire Decca Records output, from his beginnings as the Elks Rendez-Vous Band with Rodney Sturgis on vocals in December 1938 to his last sessions for the label in January 1954.

For the first time, serious music fans who had only heard at best a dozen or so of Louie's "greatest hits" from his mid-1940s prime on compilations could grasp the full measure and breadth of Louie's unstinting musical polish as it was buffed to a shine from the late 1930s through the mid-1950s. It goes much above and beyond his well-known novelty tunes—from instrumentals to ballads, from blues to orchestral works—and Louie handles it all with incredible aplomb. Most impressive through the hours of listening is the unending spark Louie gives to even the most obscure unreleased cut. There's the suspicion some of the material would falter in lesser hands, but rarely does Louie make a misstep in the more than fifteen years of collected works.

The ninth disc collects the six titles that Louie and Ella Fitzgerald recorded for Decca—1946's "Stone Cold Dead in the Market"/"Petootie Pie," 1949's "Baby, It's Cold Outside"/"Don't Cry, Cry Baby" and 1950's "Ain't Nobody's Business But My Own"/"I'll Never Be Free," plus an unreleased take of "Petootie Pie"—and puts the icing on the cake.

By the early 1950s, when Louie had left Decca after millions in sales, his old bandmate and paramour Ella Fitzgerald had racked up some twenty-two million units sold herself. When she died in 1996, Fitzgerald had won more than a dozen Grammys, been honored by presidents and long been a known name to even non-musical households. Despite their brief romance, collaboration together with Chick Webb and numerous duets over the years when they were both solo stars, unmentioned in all but the most detailed obituary was the Jordan name.

Classic Tympany Five songs can still be heard regularly on movies, television and commercials. A breakfast cereal would use Louie's "Barnyard Boogie" and its lyrics "Oink! Oink! Moo!" to contrast breakfast meats with its healthiness; the 1992 film *A League of Their Own* would use "Choo Choo Ch'Boogie" in a train-traveling sequence. Louie's "nobody here but us chickens" catchphrase would extend beyond the galaxy when uttered by Captain James T. Kirk upon encountering a desolate planet in the first season of TV's *Star Trek*—among many cultural references to Louie's songs over the decades.

Food and eating montages in film, TV programs and commercials alike would find treasure in Louie's trove of food songs—as did those holding the publishing rights to the various Tympany Five songs. This has also helped keep Louie's songs going, even as his name fades. Many music fans around the world will recognize song titles like "Choo Choo Ch'Boogie," "Caldonia" or "Ain't Nobody Here But Us Chickens" who do not know the name Louis Jordan.

Bob Dylan's mid-1970s Rolling Thunder Revue tours and film were cultural touchstones; feature performer "Ramblin'" Jack Elliot included "Salt Pork, West Virginia" in his sets. In addition to Dylan's "Open the Door, Homer" Basement Tapes homage and its sing-along refrain, "Open the door, Richard, I've heard it said before, but I ain't gonna hear it said no more," Dylan has regularly featured Louie's music on his satellite radio program.

"Let the Good Times Roll" is prominently featured in a scene in 1980's *The Blues Brothers*. The recently reunited brothers, Elwood (Dan Aykroyd) and Jake (John Belushi), return to Elwood's apartment, and Elwood puts the song on the record player. Next thing he knows, Jake is sleeping like a baby—in Elwood's bed. The record player's needle is still cycling on the record in the morning.

The 2003 film *Elf* likewise features a Louie song in a memorable scene. "Baby, It's Cold Outside" is sung by Zooey Deschanel with Will Farrell, though it appears on the soundtrack as a duet with Deschanel and Leon Redbone, who also appeared in *Elf*. "Baby, It's Cold Outside" has had a resurgent afterlife, being sung by other such odd couples over the decades as Mae West and Rock Hudson, Ann-Margret and Al Hirt, Dionne Warwick and Ray Charles, Doris Day and Dean Martin, Barry Manilow and K.T. Oslin, James Taylor and Natalie Cole, Willie Nelson and Norah Jones, Rod Stewart and Dolly Parton and actors Selma Blair and Rainn Wilson (for a TV commercial).

In Arkansas, attempts have been made to make the state an island of Louis Jordan celebration in a nation awash in indifference.

In the 1970s and 1980s, Windy Austin, a regionally influential musician in the northwest Arkansas college town of Fayetteville, nearly single-handedly re-introduced Louie's music to a new, educated hippie generation with his bands Zorro and the Blue Footballs and the Hot House Tomato Boys and their often profane but always musically adept (with sax player) takes on "Ain't Nobody Here But Us Chickens" and similar fare.

Another event, Little Rock's Louis Jordan Tribute, would help bring Louie's name back into the musical pantheon of the handful of best-known native performers—most of whom were influenced by Louie anyway. The first Louis Jordan Tribute concert event was held on July 8, 1997, on what would have been Louie's eighty-ninth birthday, in Little Rock (founded and hosted in proud disclosure by your author).

"Good times roll at Jordan tribute," the *Brinkley Argus* newspaper proclaimed the following day. But despite some regional press in Dallas, St. Louis and Memphis and being recognized by the U.S. Library of Congress's "Local Legacies" program, the annual event didn't attract much attention outside the state.

Above the fold in the same issue of the *Brinkley Argus*, however, a more ominous headline appeared: "Union Pacific gathering bids to demolish historic depot." Union Pacific Railroad representatives confirmed in the article that contractors had visited the city's historic Rock Island depot to submit bids for demolition.

The first Louis Jordan Tribute concert in Little Rock in 1997 marked what would have been Jordan's eighty-ninth birthday.

144

This, despite Brinkley City Council denying the request the previous fall and the local Central Delta Historical Society noting the depot's connections to Brinkley's origins as a railroad town, host to the likes of President Theodore Roosevelt shortly after its completion in 1912, and its consideration as a home for a museum for the area. Union Pacific public affairs director John Bromley said in the article that railroad personnel had ruled that the depot was both beyond repair as well as being too close to the tracks to be donated to an outside entity.

Yet that is exactly what happened. The Central Delta Historical Society turned the depot into a museum for the area. In 2003, the first Choo Choo Ch'Boogie Delta Music Festival was held on museum grounds and was so named to acknowledge Brinkley's train history, the depot itself and, of course, the city's most famous son and one of his most popular songs. Festival T-shirts appropriated the "Choo Choo Ch'Boogie" sheet music illustration of a grinning steam train balling the jack with piano keys substituting for train tracks, music notes wafting from the train's smokestack while nearby birds look on in awe.

The Louis Jordan Tribute events continued to be held in Little Rock for more than a decade, with Arkansas-connected performers such as Levon Helm (who performed Louie's songs throughout his career, including organizing 1975's Grammy-winning *The Muddy Waters Woodstock Album*, produced by Hot Springs native Henry Glover and including "Caldonia" and "Let the Good Times Roll"), Lucinda Williams, Al Bell (a Brinkley native and Stax Records executive and producer who says he's a distant relative of Louie's), Trout Fishing in America, CeDell Davis, John Weston, Jim Dickinson and many local musicians, dignitaries and visual artists participating in various ways. Tribute concert proceeds eventually funded a bust of Louie playing the sax, sculpted by Little Rock artist John Deering—the artist who, with his team of sculptors, also created statues of Central High School's Little Rock Nine on state capitol grounds. The bust of Louie resides in the Brinkley train depot–turned-museum as part of the facility's Jordan display and collection. As a boy, Louie had ferried travelers' luggage for tips from the depot. The Brinkley museum's director, Bill Sayger, appears briefly in the *Is You Is: A Louis Jordan Story* documentary cleaning the gravestone of Jim Jordan. It was a symbolic moment that points to his stewardship, along with several others, of the area's history, where the Louis Jordan name looms larger than in most locales. Thomas and Katie Jacques, editors and publishers of the *Brinkley Argus* newspaper in the 1990s and 2000s and knowledgeable music fans, also helped re-introduce the man to the area with numerous articles about Louie, the Jordan tributes, local preservation and tourism efforts and more.

Above: Louis Jordan's hometown of Brinkley, Arkansas, recognized Jordan and the area's musical heritage with its Choo Choo Ch'Boogie Delta Music Festival.

Opposite: The second-annual Louis Jordan Tribute concert/conference in Little Rock featured Louie's widow, Martha, as guest of honor.

Louie was inducted into the Arkansas Entertainers Hall of Fame in October 1998 as the hall inaugurated its new, permanent home in the Pine Bluff Convention Center. Pine Bluff is considered the hometown of early Tympany Five producer J. Mayo "Ink" Williams as well as Casey Bill Weldon, original singer of Louie's early hits "I'm Gonna Move to the Outskirts of Town" and "Somebody Done Changed the Lock on My Door." (Neither Williams nor Weldon has yet merited entrance into the hall, however.)

Martha Jordan attended the Arkansas Entertainers Hall of Fame ceremony and provided what the *Arkansas Democrat-Gazette* called the evening's "most emotional moment" in her acceptance speech, when she was also presented with a portrait of Louie painted by Little Rock artist Jana Frost. The painting hung in Martha's Las Vegas apartment for years thereafter. Martha had also visited the state of Arkansas that July as guest of honor at the second Louis Jordan Tribute, recognizing what would have been Louie's ninetieth birthday in Little Rock—even joining a band onstage to reminisce and sing a bit of "I'll Never Be Free," proclaiming that Louie's spirit was in the house on that hot summer night.

Later that fall, a group of well-meaning music lovers in St. Louis, Missouri, fronted by radio station KDHX-FM 88, led a drive to install a bench, tree and memorial plaque next to Louie's headstone. One fundraiser, held at St. Louis's City Museum, actually lost money. Further, no one had ever asked Martha Jordan her thoughts on such changes to her family's graveside (the Weavers), and the idea was eventually scrapped.

Louis Jordan was named an American Music Master by the Rock and Roll Hall of Fame and was the subject of a week's worth of study and music on October 3–10, 1999, that included Bo Diddley, Ruth Brown, Johnnie Johnson, Bobby Rush and Bennie Ross "Hank" Crawford of Memphis, who had been Ray Charles's musical director in the early 1960s. Also performing were B.B. King (plugging his new Louis Jordan tribute album), Al Kooper, Southside Johnny and the Asbury Jukes, Big Bad Voodoo Daddy (one of the torch-bearing "swing revival" bands of the era, even playing that year's Super Bowl halftime festivities), your author and more. Louie's honoring was the Rock and Roll Hall of Fame's fourth annual in its American Music Masters Series; previous honorees had been Muddy Waters, Robert Johnson and Jimmie Rogers.

In 2008, Louie's pioneering contributions to the black film industry in America were acknowledged in part of a series of United States Postal Service stamps depicting vintage film posters. Louie's stamp showed him in his silly coat and top hat from the song "Tillie" from the *Caldonia* movie poster. It was nice timing but, as far as the U.S. Postal Service was concerned, purely coincidental that 2008 would have been Louie's 100th birthday, although prior attempts had been made over the years to get Louie on an American postage stamp for his broader musical, as opposed to film, achievements.

Also during the 2008 Louis Jordan centennial year—and Louie's birth month of July—a musical based on Louie's life and music premiered in his home state to sold-out audiences. Called *Jump! The Louis Jordan Story* (and written by your author), the play's debut featured Martha as guest of honor. "[*Jump!*] shows off the beloved musician in the best light, namely to have a hot band and great singers run through the highlights of Jordan's amazing catalog of hits," reported Little Rock's *Arkansas Democrat-Gazette* newspaper. "And what incredible, funny and brimming-with-life-and-then-some songs they are."

Closing the review, reporter Werner Trieschmann noted, "The audience Sunday night gave the show a standing ovation and the crowd could hardly keep still during some of the livelier tunes. Louis Jordan has that effect on people." And, might as well include the article's kicker: "Thank goodness Stephen Koch is around to remind us."

Despite Louie's unmatched chart success, his profound influence on those who themselves became the musically influential and the postmortem efforts to recognize and celebrate his innovative music, Louie remains mostly off the pantheon of American musical greats.

And even as Louie was being paid tribute, being inducted into halls of fame and being featured on a U.S. postage stamp, his Aunt Lizzie's house on Brinkley's Main Street—where Louie spent most of his life as a boy—was falling down.

A faded homemade sign and the crumbling dwelling in Brinkley serve as a leitmotif in the documentary film *Is You Is: A Louis Jordan Story*, which premiered at the Hot Springs International Documentary Film Festival in October 2008.

With the home's prime location on Brinkley's Main Street, it was more the generally stagnant eastern Arkansas Delta economy that had helped preserve the structure for a full decade into the twenty-first century, rather than the building's historic status as the childhood home of one of the innovative greats of American popular music.

As years passed, various officials from the City of Brinkley pondered their options on the Reid family's place, including having the privately owned property condemned and having the building moved to the grounds of the city's museum—the former train depot that had narrowly avoided the call of the wrecking ball itself.

In the meantime, however, there became nothing left to save.

'ARKANSONGS' PRESENTS
The Ninth Annual

LOUIS JORDAN
TRIBUTE

Featuring:

JIM DICKINSON
BRIAN PARTON (N-ville Rebels)
GREG SPRADLIN OUTFIT
THE BUG TUSSLE BOYS
THE MONKS
BEN MANATT & more

JULY 7, 2005
North Little Rock
Cornerstone Pub, 312 Main St.

$5 Suggested donation benefits Louis Jordan Memorial, c/o Bank of Brinkley, Brinkley, AR 72021 USA

FUN FILLED! JIVE JAMMED! PEP PACKED!
IS YOU IS OR IS YOU AIN'T GONNA BE THERE?

Left: By the 2005 Louis Jordan Tribute concert, the late performer Jim Dickinson was headlining, and the bulk of the funds for a bust of Jordan to be placed in his Arkansas hometown of Brinkley had been raised.

Below: Seen here in the late 1990s, Louis Jordan's boyhood home on Main Street in Brinkley eventually crumbled due to neglect, despite intermittent efforts to preserve it. *Author photo.*

A bust of Brinkley, Arkansas' most famous son, Louis Jordan, can be found in the city's museum, a former train station where Louie was said to have ferried passengers' bags for tips as a lad. *Courtesy Doug Holloway, Brinkley Argus.*

And in some way, the fate of the building seems appropriate. Wood rots, buildings fall.

Songs—and performers—rise and fall off the charts by the very nature of chart-keeping and including the adjective "popular" before "music."

The name Louis Jordan hasn't weathered well, but songs like "Caldonia Boogie," "Let the Good Times Roll," "Choo Choo Ch'Boogie," "Saturday Night Fish Fry" and many more continue to be heard, decades later, in all sorts of places all around the world.

Or, to paraphrase Louie in his 1944 number-one song "Mop! Mop!"— about a musician commissioned to "find a riff that's new"—Louie is gone, but his jive lives on, and it still is making history. Mop! Mop!

The End

BIBLIOGRAPHY

Adams, Berle. Interviews, 2001–2006.

Adams, Berle, with Gordon Cohn. *A Sucker for Talent: From Cocktail Lounges to MCA: 50 Years as Agent, Manager, and Executive*. N.p.: self-published, 1995.

Armstrong, Louis. *Satchmo: My Life in New Orleans*. New York: Prentice-Hall, 1954.

Arnold, Tom. Interviews, 2011–2013.

Berry, Chuck. *Chuck Berry: The Autobiography*. New York: Simon & Schuster, 1987.

Billboard magazine, July 22, 1944.

Brazzel, Kyle. "Eleven Inducted as Hall Enters Its Permanent Home." *Arkansas Democrat-Gazette*, October 11, 1998.

Brown, James. *I Feel Good: A Memoir of a Life of Soul*. London: Penguin Books, 2005.

Brown, James, with Bruce Tucker. *James Brown, an Autobiography*. New York: Thunder's Mouth Press, 1986.

Calvin, Dolores. "Louis Jordan Consults Horoscope on 41ˢᵗ Birthday; He Is Shy but Clinging Type." *Arkansas State Press*, July 8, 1949.

Chicago Defender. "Louis Jordan Stabbed by Wife; Near Death." February 1, 1947.

Chilton, John. *Let the Good Times Roll: The Story of Louis Jordan and His Music*. Ann Arbor: University of Michigan Press, 1992.

Clancy, Sean. "Let the Good Times Roll: Louis Jordan and Brinkley." *Central Delta Historical Journal*, August 1998.

Down Beat, February 4, 1960.

————. November 1937.

————. "Health Forces Louis Jordan into Retirement." February 8, 1952.

————. "'I'm Not Changing Style,' Says a Fretful Jordan." June 3, 1953.

————. "Jordan Attracts Huge Crowds at Kaycee Dance." September 21, 1951.

————. "Jordan Doesn't Like It, but He Plays, Anyhow." December 15, 1948.

————. "Jordan Makes Florida History." December 3, 1947.

————. "Louis Jordan Recovering from Stabbing." February 12, 1947.

Escott, Colin, with Martin Hawkins. *Good Rockin' Tonight: Sun Records and the Birth of Rock 'n' Roll*. New York: St. Martin's Press, 1991.

Feather, Leonard. "Louis Jordan's Big Band Pleasant, Should Do Well." *Down Beat*, January 2, 1952.

————. "Louis Jordan: The Good Times Still Roll." *Down Beat*, May 29, 1969.

————. "The Return of Louis Jordan." *Los Angeles Times*, April 27, 1973.

Hickey, Scott. "Fundraiser to Help Give Musician His Due." *South County (Missouri) Journal*, November 29, 1998.

Jacques, Thomas. "Good Times Roll at Jordan Tribute." *Brinkley (AR) Argus*, July 9, 1997.

———. "Jordan House Continues to Stand after Discussion at Council Meeting." *Brinkley (AR) Argus*, August 21, 1998.

———. "Union Pacific Gathering Bids to Demolish Historic Depot." *Brinkley (AR) Argus,* July 9, 1997.

Jobe Pierce, Patricia. *The Ultimate Elvis: Elvis Presley Day by Day*. New York: Simon & Schuster, 1994.

Jones, Quincy. *Q: The Autobiography of Quincy Jones*. New York: Random House, 2001.

Jordan, Martha. Interviews, 1998–2008.

Jordan, Martha, with Edith A. Coleman. *The Debutante Who Went Astray*. Lee's Summit, MO: E.L.M. Institute Publishers, 2005.

King, B.B., with David Ritz. *Blues All Around Me: The Autobiography of B.B. King*. New York: Avon Books, 1996.

Koch, S. "Endangered in Brinkley." *Arkansas Democrat-Gazette,* July 8, 1999.

———. "Louis Jordan Gets His Due." *Little Rock Free Press*, February 24, 1995.

Masouri, John. *Wailing Blues: The Story of Bob Marley's Wailers.* London: Omnibus Press, 2008.

McGee, David. *B.B. King: There Is Always One More Time*. San Francisco: Backbeat, 2005.

Mezzrow, Mezz, and Bernard Wolfe. *Really the Blues*. New York: Citadel Underground, 1946.

Musician. "Sonny Rollins." May 1988.

Newsweek magazine, July 8, 1946.

Nicholson, Stuart. *Ella Fitzgerald: A Biography of the First Lady of Jazz.* New York: Simon & Schuster, 1994.

Nisenson, Eric. *Open Sky: Sonny Rollins and His World of Improvisation.* New York: St. Martin's Press, 2000.

O'Neal, Jim. "Louis Jordan (obituary)." *Living Blues,* March/April 1975.

Otis, Johnny. "Louis Jordan, the Otis Tapes: 1." *Blues Unlimited,* February/March 1974.

Parker, Suzi. "Arkansan 'Real Deal' in R&B Land." *Memphis Commercial Appeal,* July 29, 2001.

Pegg, Bruce. *Brown-Eyed Handsome Man: The Life & Hard Times of Chuck Berry.* New York: Routledge, 2002.

Porter, Eugene. Interviews, 1998–2008.

Reed, Roy. *Faubus: The Life and Times of an American Prodigal.* Fayetteville: University of Arkansas Press, 1997.

Sullivan, James. *The Hardest Working Man: How James Brown Saved the Soul of America.* New York: Gotham Books, 2008.

Trieschmann, Werner. "Koch's Tribute Jumps with Jordan Tunes." *Arkansas Democrat-Gazette,* July 21, 2008.

Wilford, Red. "Louis Jordan Passes in Los Angeles, Famed Musician to Be Buried Here." *St. Louis Argus,* February 6, 1975.

INDEX